W9-DEW-053

Contents

Using Mirrors to Manipulate Fabric Design

Placing mirrors at a 90° angle shows four repeats of the motif.

A 45° angle shows eight repeats of the motif.

A 60° angle shows six repeats, which could be made into a hexagon design as shown.

"Why are you cutting up perfectly good fabric, just to sew it together again?" my neighbor used to ask. Well, besides enjoying patchwork and quilting, I have an excellent reason. Using a set of angled mirrors, I can discover intriguing designs in printed fabrics, and I can manipulate the printed shapes into totally new designs by cutting up and rearranging them. I become, in effect, the designer of my own fabric, without lifting a brush or pen. And the ongoing "discovery" of new designs is nothing but fun!

The mirror technique works with a wide range of print styles. Learn how to turn a big fish print into a visual enigma, or a large, loud paisley into gently swirling stars. You'll never look at prints the same way again.

Mirrors can also help you plan quilt borders, block designs, quilting designs, and entire quilt-top designs. Use them to see what blocks look like repeated, rotated, or set on point.

Take a traditional block design and "extend" it to create a complex-looking original design. Discover "hidden" shapes within traditional blocks to make unique and wonderfully complementary border designs. Find the best way to turn a corner with print borders, pieced borders, or with quilting designs. Learn how to adapt any printed motif to a square, round, or triangular quilting design.

Once you start playing with mirrors, you won't want to put them down. You'll discover a whole new world of quilt design.

The best way to introduce yourself to this technique is to start playing with a set of mirrors. Many quilt shops carry small sets of mirrors, or you may order them from Valentine Designs, 7305 Foxtree Cove, Austin, TX 78750, $5.00 plus $1.50 shipping and handling. Two mirrors are taped together along one edge, so they can be opened to any angle. When they are placed on top of a printed design, the portion of the design isolated between the two mirrors is reflected in them a number of times, depending on the angle of the opening.

Open the mirrors until the sides form a right angle (90°). If you place them at this angle on a single flower, you will see four flowers (fig. 1).

Now close the mirrors halfway. This is a 45° angle, the correct angle for eight repeats or Eight-Point Star designs (fig. 2).

Open the mirrors a bit more to a 60° angle, the correct angle for hexagons and Six-Point Stars (fig. 3).

We'll cover accuracy later, but for now you have an approximate idea of how to angle the mirrors. Find an interesting shape in a large-scale print and place the angled mirrors on it. Looking into the mirrors, you will see several repeats of this shape and what it might look like as a pieced block. Move the mirrors to see what other designs you can form with the print.

The mirror technique gives you a general idea of how an image will look when it's repeated. But if you've isolated an asymmetrical shape, don't be fooled into thinking that every other one will be reversed, as you see in the mirrors. Instead, the motif in each wedge of your pieced block will be identical. See "Mirror Image versus True Repetition" on page 10.

You will cut out identical segments of the print throughout your yardage to re-create the kaleidoscopic image in the mirrors. Be sure to read through the fabric suggestions and look at the examples and the finished quilts to see how the mirrored motifs translate into pieced designs. I hope you'll be as excited as I am about this technique.

Selecting Fabrics for Mirror-Print Designs

I have always enjoyed the dramatic colors and designs in large-scale prints. But, with the exception of an occasional floral print, most of the large-scale prints, especially the wild-and-crazy novelty prints, seemed unsuitable for patchwork designs. And indeed, when cut up into small pieces in the traditional way, large-scale prints can lose their color continuity and cause a splotchy look in a quilt. The mirrored-print technique provides an exciting way to use these prints in quilts.

Take a tour through your local quilt shops and fabric stores and you're bound to find some great large-scale prints. To see things from a new perspective, get out of the calico section and browse through the dress or decorator prints—maybe even look at the juvenile section.

Prints you never thought of using for quilts may be just what you need for this technique—a bold fish print, wonderful fruits, vegetables, seashells, birds, a variety of playful, cartoonlike animals, or detailed, realistic wildlife. You may find prints depicting various sports and hobbies—golf, baseball, hunting, and fishing; nautical themes; even sewing implements. There are florals everywhere. And, depending on the season, you may find romantic, antique Valentine scenes; colorful harvest prints; or a wide variety of Christmas prints.

The basic idea of the mirror technique is to find an interesting shape in the print, isolate it, and repeat it to form an intriguing new design. Many times, the most interesting shapes are portions of motifs that are not readily identifiable when looking at a print. That is why mirrors are such an important part of the design process. By moving a hinged set of mirrors across the print, you can discover a multitude of hidden designs. A flower with a trailing vine may be transformed into a bouquet with a spiraling Celtic design in the background, or a playful animal may suddenly pinwheel around a center hexagon.

The success of this technique depends upon your choice of fabric. Some prints produce wonderful designs, while some only result in wasted effort. Look at the examples, follow the suggestions, and play with your mirrors on any fabric you are considering. If you can find a variety of exciting shapes, colors, and designs hidden in the print, it has good potential for this technique.

I like the properties of 100% cotton fabric. It has enough body to hold its shape but also has a little "give" to it. Regular quilting-weight cottons are best, but decorator fabrics may work too, as long as they aren't too heavy or stiff to make the intricate block designs. Be wary of off-price fabrics that might be seconds. These often have irregularities in the print that make them unsuitable for the technique.

You *don't* need the same prints shown in this book. The samples are simply to demonstrate how you might use a particular *type* of print, so that you can see how to apply the mirror technique.

Desirable Traits in a Print

To create a dramatic design, start with a dramatic print. Look for prints with the following desirable traits:

- Medium to large scale
- Multicolored
- Distinct or high contrast
- Featuring several different shapes or motifs

Medium- to Large-Scale Prints

To use the mirror technique, select prints with fairly large motifs so you can isolate interesting parts of the design. With a small print or one in which the motifs are too close together, extraneous parts of the print may appear in the template and confuse the image you are trying to isolate. However, if the print meets most of the other criteria and is simply a bit too small in scale for your block pattern, you may be able to adjust the scale of your pattern. (See "Adjusting Scale: Drafting" on page 18.)

In figure 4, you can see that distinct parts of the print can be isolated much more easily in the larger-scale prints on the right.

Multicolored Prints

To make many different-looking stars (or other shapes), use a print with several colors in it. The colors should be "clustered" or placed somewhat irregularly throughout the print. If each motif in the print contains all of the colors, the print is too homogeneous, and your stars may look too much the same to be worth the trouble of cutting out all those separate pieces.

Study the individual prints on the left in figure 5. The motifs are composed of very few colors and they all contain essentially the same ones. That doesn't mean they won't work at all. You might get a few interesting designs but would quickly run out of options if you're trying to create several different-looking blocks. Or the variations would be so subtle, it would hardly be worth your time and effort.

The prints on the right would produce a greater number of different-looking blocks. Because of their greater variety of colors, pieces cut from different areas of the print would not always contain the same combinations of colors.

4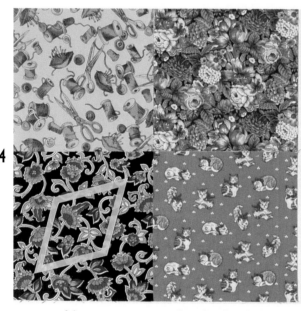

Portions of the print are more easily isolated in the larger-scale prints on the right.

5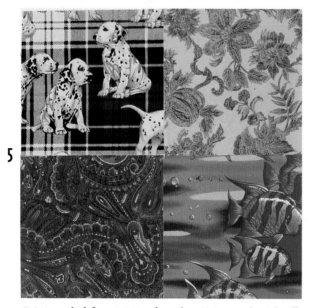

Prints on the left contain too few colors. Prints on the right offer a greater variety.

Distinct or High-Contrast Prints

The prints that work best for the mirror-print technique have well-defined motifs, rather than soft, water-color shapes that blend into the background. Prints with dramatic color and/or value contrast between the figure and the background work well. Background color showing between the motifs also helps to separate and define the shapes. The prints on the left in figure 6 do not have clear, sharp, well-defined shapes. The prints on the right have distinct motifs and would result in more dramatic designs.

Value contrast is also important. Although you may be able to see different motifs and colors up close, low-contrast prints may become "muddy" or may even read as solid colors when viewed from several feet away. You wouldn't want to piece intricate printed stars only to have them look like solids! Use a reducing glass or the Ruby Beholder™, blur your vision by squinting, or view the print from a distance to judge its suitability. The prints on the left in figure 7 have low contrast. Those on the right have higher contrast between the figure and the background and work better with this technique.

6

Soft blending colors and shapes on the left do not work as well as sharply defined prints on the right.

7

Low-contrast prints on the left do not show up as well as high-contrast prints on the right.

Prints with Several Different Shapes or Motifs

If the print contains only one general shape or motif (different-colored apples, for example), it will be difficult to create dramatically different blocks. After all that work, your blocks may not look much different than your uncut fabric. A print with a variety of different shapes will produce more interesting designs (fig. 8).

Some fabrics that are not ideal as the main fabric for the mirror technique can be used successfully with other fabrics. If you can only get a few designs from a fabric, try using it in a quilt with other prints. Christmas prints, in particular, usually contain few motifs and few colors in one print, but can be used with other fabrics for more variety.

Remember to take your mirrors to the fabric store because playing with mirrors on fabric will help you see designs you might have missed.

The abstract floral print in figure 9 contains few colors, but there is such variety in shapes, motifs, and values that quite a few designs can be created from it. The Southwest print shows only moccasins, but there are so many different shapes of moccasins, with different-colored decorations, that distinctly different designs can be formed.

The shape you are trying to isolate will be easier to see and have a more dramatic effect if you follow these guidelines when you select prints. If you are unsure about whether a print will work, just experiment with your mirrors.

Categories of Prints

Let's look at some categories of prints that work successfully with the mirror technique. Remember the four desirable qualities—large scale, high contrast, different colors, different shapes.

Large Florals: The greater the variety of colors and shapes you use, the more variety you can achieve in your block designs.

A manufacturer-coordinated group of fabrics offers a whole range of possibilities, but beware of looking too well matched.

Stripes or Border Prints: Border prints usually have frequent repeats but a limited variety of motifs. Use them to create additional, different-looking design blocks.

Place your mirrors sideways, across stripes, to design a hexagon or octagon.

Juvenile Prints: It's fun to create a puzzle for a child by using a large piece of uncut fabric on the back of the quilt and challenging him to find the portion of the print from which each block design was created.

Southwest Prints: It is easy to mix two or three prints together since they often contain some of the same colors.

Seasonal Prints: Large-scale seasonal prints work well as long as there are enough different shapes and color concentrations in the print.

Tropical Prints: These are great sources for bright colors and wild designs.

Novelty Prints: A wide variety of novelty prints is always available. There are nautical prints, sewing implements, fans, hat boxes, furniture—even Elvis prints! Any design you can imagine has probably been printed on fabric. Try combining prints with similar themes and colors.

Another source of suitable large-scale prints is fabric specifically designed for appliqué motifs, pillow panels, or preprinted quilt blocks.

8

Prints with few shapes will not yield as many different designs as prints with many different shapes.

9

A good variety in some qualities may compensate for a lack of variety in others.

Remember to check the decorator fabrics too, since almost every color combination is available there. Choose only compatible-weight cottons, not heavy or stiff fabrics.

When a symmetrical design emanates from the center (hinge) of the mirrors, what you see is what you get.

With an asymmetrical design, or one emanating from the side, what you see is not necessarily what you get.

Your local quilt or fabric stores have prints similar to the ones pictured in the various categories here. Don't expect to find the exact same prints, but don't worry. You've seen the general types of prints that work well with this technique, and when in doubt, play with your mirrors.

Mirror-Image versus True Repetition

If the motif you have isolated is symmetrical and emanates from the center of your design (the hinge of your mirrors), you will see a fairly true reflection of what the actual quilt block will look like (fig. 10). However, if the motif is asymmetrical or oriented in one direction, what you see is not exactly what you get. Remember that a mirror shows a reflection, and in the mirror, adjacent asymmetrical shapes are reversed. The shapes you cut from your fabric are identical, and all are facing in the same direction (fig. 11).

Occasionally, you may find a fabric that contains mirror-image designs—a paisley design or figures that face right in one place and left in another (fig. 12). To determine whether one motif is a true mirror image of another, trace the motif onto your plastic template. (See "Making Templates" on page 22.) Turn the template over and place it on top of the mirror-image motif. Do the tracing lines match? Remember that adjoining portions of neighboring motifs must also match if some of them appear in the template.

Use mirror-image motifs by alternating the two orientations. In a Six-Point Star, for example, cut one diamond with the leaf swaying to the right. Then cut out a diamond with the leaf swaying to the left. Rather than a star with six identical diamonds, you will have a star with three mirror-image shapes. These do not necessarily mix well with stars of the "normal" orientation but may be worth some experimentation.

The Southwest print in figure 13 does contain some mirror-image motifs and will yield some interesting designs. But most of the print is not true mirror image, since the background images and surrounding motifs are not identical from one figure to the next. Be sure to study everything that will appear in your template shape.

You may like designs on which you can center your mirrors so that the shape emanates from the hinge of your mirrors. This results in a pleasing radial symmetry. But don't overlook the possibility of having the design originate at one side of your mirrors. This produces a wonderful swirling design, with a great sense of movement.

Examples of Mirror-Image Motifs

Abstracting the Design

For some quilts, you may want to cut the pieces so that the motif is still easily recognizable. For a child's quilt, you may want the child to see and recognize each animal in the print. Place the mirrors so that you can include the head and as much of the animal as possible, to keep its identity intact. (See "Playful Pinwheels" on page 41.)

For other quilts, a splash of color and an intriguing design may be more important. Move the mirrors around the motif at random, until you find an interesting display of color and shapes. It may no longer be a recognizable motif. This is what I call "abstracting the design" (fig. 14).

Yardage Requirements

Yardage required for your mirror-print blocks depends on the number of repeats of a particular motif in the print, rather than on the number of yards. To use a particular motif for a Six-Point Star, you would look for six exact repeats of that motif in the print. If the first complete motif on your piece of fabric is a swaying tulip, look for the next repeat of that same swaying tulip.

Motifs may appear every 6" or 12" across and/or down the fabric, or, as in some very large-scale decorator fabrics, they may appear only once or twice in every yard of fabric. If the motif you are looking for—a particular rose, for example—looks the same but is surrounded with leaves in one place and not in another, it is not a true repeat.

Study the print. Sometimes a particular motif is repeated more often than others. You may get home and find you do indeed have eight daisies but only four tulips. Stand back to get a better impression of the print in its entirety. With a little practice, you'll easily be able to see and count the repeats.

Once you know the frequency of the repeats, base the yardage required on the number of repeats in your block design. In figure 15, I want to use repeats of the toucan with the big beak. I count the number of toucans I need, keeping in mind that I may not be able to use a motif near the edge if it is not complete.

To make one star, you cut several small pieces from your fabric, leaving it looking like Swiss cheese. But making many different stars from different parts of the print does use most of the fabric.

13

This six-part block shows three mirror-image shapes, but the print is only partially mirror image.

14

Focusing on interesting colors and shapes, rather than the intended motif, can result in wonderful abstracted designs.

For some projects, you may want to see how many different-looking blocks you can get from one fabric. For other projects, you may combine two or three very different prints in colors that coordinate nicely.

Sometimes cutting out one motif destroys the one next to it. When possible, I buy double the number of repeats required. This is especially helpful if you want to make a large quilt and/or want to keep your options open. Also, it's fun to use a piece of the original print in the border or backing to point out where your great mirrored designs came from.

Troubleshooting: Help! I Don't Have Enough Repeats!

You might find a remnant or a great fabric in your stash, but there are not enough repeats for the design you had in mind. If you can't get more of the same fabric, don't panic. Be flexible and consider a design requiring fewer repeats.

Hexagons and Six-Point Stars require only six repeats. The "Nosegay" pattern on page 63 is based on an Eight-Point Star grid but requires only six diamonds. A wide variety of designs based on a four-patch grid require only four repeats. The Fan block on page 49 requires only three repeats.

If your print has only four different animals but you need six or nine different blocks, try orienting your mirrors in different directions. Place the hinge of your mirrors at the side of the animal or the back, instead of at the head. You'll achieve an entirely different design. Consider also combining two or more complementary (or contrasting) prints in your quilt top. In "Challenge Star" on page 60, I used three different prints to create the mirrored star designs.

Also, if you can't create enough blocks from your print to make the quilt size you had in mind, consider adding different alternate blocks, either pieced or plain.

Selecting Background Fabrics

The theme print and the design it forms should be the main focus of the block. Other portions of the block should be subtle prints or even solids. Subtle prints provide interesting texture to the block and help contribute to the mood of the quilt. Subtle prints are sometimes referred to as tone-on-tone prints, print solids, or near solids (fig. 16). Contrasting solids or near solids next to a print also help define shapes crisply.

This does not mean you can't use other wonderful prints in your quilts. Just be aware of their tendency to compete with your mirrored print. You may want to place solids directly adjacent to the mirrored-print pieces and use other prints selectively to accent and complement your theme print.

Pin up your work in progress and stand back several feet to get an overall view of color, design, and value. Cut out several of your mirrored designs and place them on your design wall before deciding on the background. Because you are isolating and repeating specific parts of the print, you may be radically changing the ratio of the colors in the original print. You may be emphasizing a color that appears infrequently or in small amounts in the original print. By concentrating a particular color in this way, you can create one block that is quite different from the others, either in color or in value. It's better to know before it's in your quilt. You may even be able to correct the disparity by

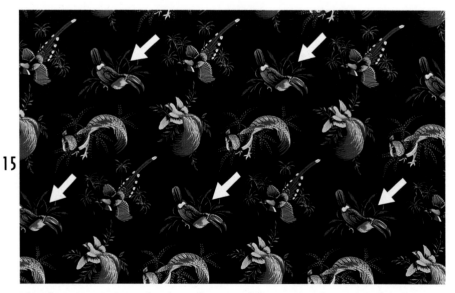

15

The white arrows point to the identical repeats of the same motif. Count the number of whole, usable repeats.

using more of that unusual color to balance the odd block.

Sometimes background pieces within a block form a frame around the mirror-print design, or you could add plain strips around your block to create a framed look. (See "Primarily Bears" on page 39.)

To "float" your mirrored designs, try placing blocks side by side and using the same background fabric in all of them. (See "A Summer Day for Doris" on page 45.) You can take this effect one step further by matching the background fabric to the background color of your theme print so that you see flowers floating on a sea of color, rather than a Six-Point Star block.

Choosing a Mirror-Print Block Design

Best Mirror-Print Block Designs

You may find a block design or a pattern and then look for some fabric that would work with it. I tend to work backwards: I wander through the quilt shops and fabric stores until I see a fabric I just love, then I start thinking about how I could use it.

The fabric itself may suggest a design. If the repeats are very infrequent or the fabric is very expensive, it may be more practical to use a design with only four or six repeats. Otherwise, I usually buy at least eight or nine repeats, sometimes more, to keep my options open.

Playing with the mirrors can help you decide on the design. If the fish motifs in the print you like are fairly large and broad but you want to incorporate as much of the motif as possible into the block design, try a six-point-center design, which has broad pieces, rather than an eight-point-center design, which has narrow pieces. Consider a kite-shaped design, which is very broad at one end, rather than a Six-Point Star, which narrows at both ends. Or, enlarge the block to enlarge the size of each piece. See "Adjusting Scale: Drafting" on page 18.

Theoretically, the mirror technique could be used anywhere two or more seams come together. But the most intriguing designs form where several seams come together at an angle, such as in the center of a star. There are dozens of traditional block designs based on the Eight-Point Star. A wide variety of Six-Point Star designs work as well. But the technique certainly isn't limited to star designs. Blocks based on four-patch units work (see "Road to Oklahoma" on page 46), and many blocks can be adapted to this technique by simply subdividing a center section into a shape composed of several pieces.

Most prints that work at all with the mirror method work in a wide variety of blocks. Be aware, however, of potential problems with asymmetrical prints. In blocks with six and eight-point centers, it doesn't seem to matter whether the print is asymmetrical—the design just swirls and looks very pleasing. But, with some blocks based on the four-patch unit, such as Blazing Star, the orientation is strongly vertical and

horizontal (with star points, in this example). If the printed motif is asymmetrical, the block may appear to lean or be off-balance (fig. 17). Prints with symmetrical motifs suit these blocks best.

Most blocks have some background pieces or other pieces that are not part of the mirrored design. These can also be an important part of your overall design by emphasizing a color in your print or by forming a secondary design.

I like to categorize the blocks by the number of repeats of the print needed to make them, using the mirrored-design technique. On pages 14 and 15 are some examples of traditional blocks or variations that work well with this technique.

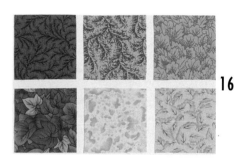

16

Using subtle prints adjacent to the mirrored prints will help calm and define the shapes.

17

Symmetrical four-patch block designs look unbalanced with asymmetrical motifs.

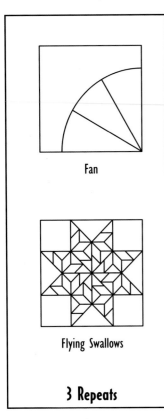

Fan

Flying Swallows

3 Repeats

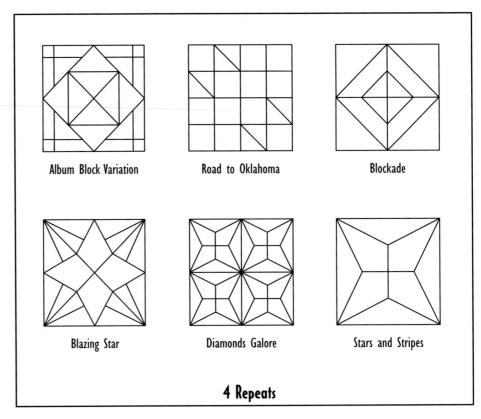

Album Block Variation

Road to Oklahoma

Blockade

Blazing Star

Diamonds Galore

Stars and Stripes

4 Repeats

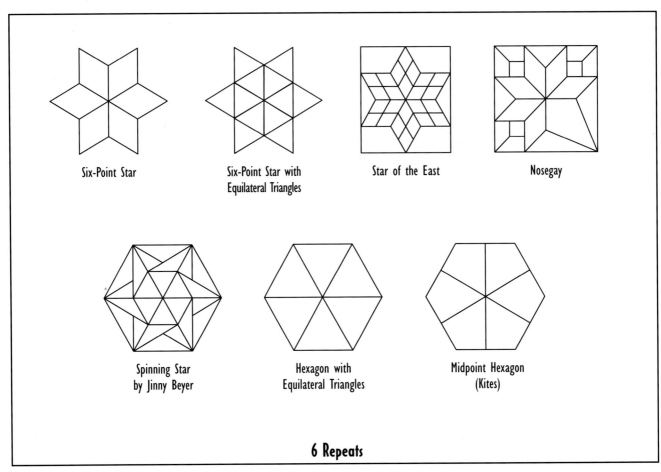

Six-Point Star

Six-Point Star with Equilateral Triangles

Star of the East

Nosegay

Spinning Star by Jinny Beyer

Hexagon with Equilateral Triangles

Midpoint Hexagon (Kites)

6 Repeats

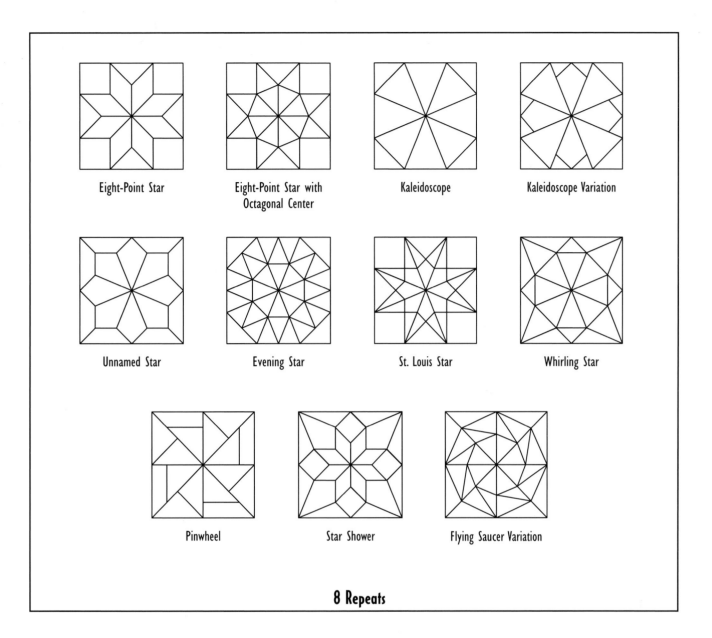

Eight-Point Star

Eight-Point Star with Octagonal Center

Kaleidoscope

Kaleidoscope Variation

Unnamed Star

Evening Star

St. Louis Star

Whirling Star

Pinwheel

Star Shower

Flying Saucer Variation

8 Repeats

Altering Traditional Blocks

Many traditional block designs can be altered to accommodate mirrored designs. A square in the center of a block can be transformed into a star, a kaleidoscope, a pinwheel, a four-patch unit, or a quarter-square triangle unit (fig. 18). Any of these smaller shapes can be made using the mirror technique.

Sometimes, the central space can be made larger by pushing the design lines out or by dropping out some lines from the center of the block. Then a mirror-friendly shape can be inserted (figs. 19, 20).

Even though you usually want a block with pieces that come together in the center, don't limit yourself to traditional block designs. Create your own design!

Nonadjacent Mirror-Print Designs

Another interesting use of printed motifs, although not dependent on the use of mirrors, is repeating the design in nonadjacent areas. This involves cutting out identical portions of a print using a plastic template and placing them in various nonadjacent parts of the block design. This technique can be combined with the mirror technique for interesting effects or can be used in portions of alternate blocks to repeat some of the printed motif without creating a too-busy block (fig. 21).

Notice the "Window Trellis" quilt on page 43, where the central part of the nosegay was made using the mirror technique, while the squares between the petals are nonadjacent repeats of another motif.

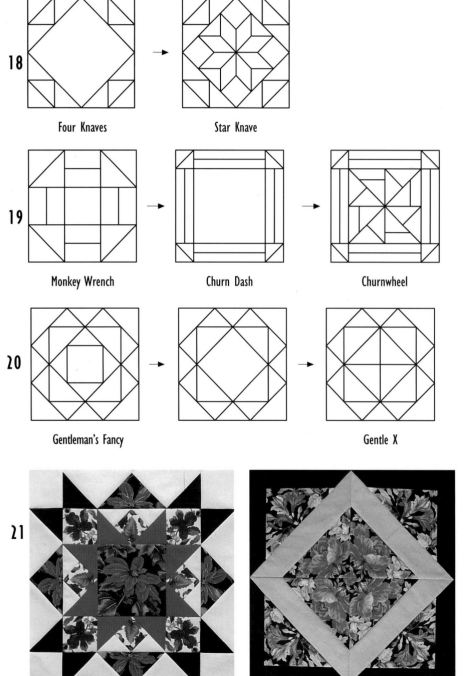

18 Four Knaves → Star Knave

19 Monkey Wrench → Churn Dash → Churnwheel

20 Gentleman's Fancy → Gentle X

21

At left, identical motifs are repeated in nonadjacent parts of the block. At right, the center forms a mirrored design, while the corners are nonadjacent repetitions of the design.

Choosing Alternate Blocks and Settings

Experiment with various settings for your blocks. If the mirrored-print section of the block is surrounded by a calmer background fabric, you may be able to set the blocks right next to each other. But sometimes the bold, swirling designs are too busy to set side by side, and look much better when separated by sashing strips or set on point.

Consider adding alternate blocks. Plain, unpieced, or simplified blocks can calm and separate your designs. Quilt them to add textural interest. Add interesting secondary designs with alternate blocks of a different pieced design from your mirror-print block (fig. 22). In "City Slicker Stars" on page 66, Mexican Star blocks between the Eight-Point Star blocks form an interesting crisscross design.

In general, use alternate blocks that line up with the dominant design lines of your main block. For example, Nine Patch blocks can be redrafted based on an Eight-Point Star grid in order to match the points of other star design blocks. The changes appear very slight, but the seams and points are more compatible with your main blocks.

Some of the block designs provided for the mirror technique can also be used as alternate blocks. To experiment, I usually trace a block and move it next to my mirror-print block drawing to see how they connect and what secondary designs form. Add, subtract, or change design lines to make your blocks more com-patible, add interest, simplify the design, or make piecing easier.

Sometimes, by manipulating the coloration of adjacent blocks, you can make one block appear to connect or flow into another. (See "Christmas by Stars and Candlelight" on page 37.)

To set square blocks on point (a diagonal setting), square off the quilt with triangles at the sides and corners (fig. 23). The straight of grain should always be along the outside edges of the quilt. There are simple, math-ematical formulas for determining the size of the triangles required. For the corner triangles, you already know the length of the long side of the triangle, since it's the same size as the finished side of your block. Divide this mea-surement by 1.414 to find the length of the short sides of the triangle. Then, add ⅞" for seam allowances. Cut a square this size, then cut it in half di-agonally for two corner triangles (fig. 24a).

For side setting triangles, you know the length of the short side of the triangle, which is also the same as the finished side of your block. Multi-ply this figure by 1.414 to find the length of the long side of the triangle. Add 1¼" for seam allowances. Cut a square of fabric that size, and cut it twice diagonally to yield four triangles with the straight grain along the long-est side (fig. 24b).

An easy way to set hexagons is to turn them so the flat sides are at the top and they touch at the points. Fill in the spaces with triangular setting blocks as in "Tropical Twist" on page 39. The setting triangle is one-sixth of the original hexagon. Piece the blocks and triangles in diagonal rows to avoid set-in seams (fig. 25).

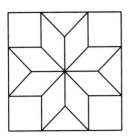

Make main block Eight-Point Star in mirrored print. 22

Make alternate block with added X shape in solids.

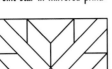

Corner triangle

23

Side triangle

Plain alternate blocks between the pieced blocks calm a design.

(a) Corner Triangles   (b) Side Triangles   24a, b

←straight of grain→   ←straight of grain→

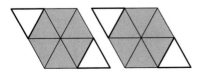

25

Setting triangles are ⅙ of the hexagon blocks.

26

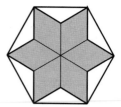

Six-Point Star
with Half Diamonds

27

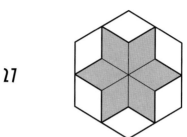

Six-Point Star
with Full Diamonds

Six-Point Stars become hexagons with either a half-diamond shape or a full-diamond shape between the star points (figs. 26, 27). Or, the star itself can be the finished block unit and set with an alternate block, such as a hexagon or a diamond shape.

Another approach is to interlace the stars. (See "Spinning Star Galaxy" on page 34.) This works best when the outer star points are not part of the busy mirrored design.

The hexagons or stars can be arranged into larger hexagons or elongated hexagons, or custom-fit triangles can be added to square off the quilt. As you can see from some of the samples in this book, not all quilts are

square. Don't be afraid of making an odd-shaped quilt, such as a hexagon. Directions for hanging an odd-shaped quilt are given on page 32.

Adjusting Scale: Drafting

As you can see in the previous block diagrams, the area for the mirrored portion can vary greatly in size. Draft your own block in a size compatible with your print, or decide on a block size and look for an appropriately sized print. Isolate a single motif or enjoy the way the motif flows into the adjoining piece (fig. 28).

If the print is so small that the motifs you intend to feature are just "floating" amid other motifs, you will need to scale down the pattern, choose a pattern with smaller pieces, or choose a larger print. If your print is so large that you can only capture a small portion of it in the pattern piece, you may want to redraft the pattern to a larger size or choose a pattern with larger pieces (fig. 29).

Most of the patterns in this book are based on either a four-patch unit, an Eight-Point Star, or a Six-Point Star or hexagon. For most of the blocks, you begin by drafting a grid and then complete the various designs by drawing lines to connect points on the grid. Draft on graph paper to ensure accuracy.

28

A single motif is isolated on the right, while on the left, the motif merges to form a wreath.

29

At left, the print is too small for a template this size, while at right, the print is a little too big.

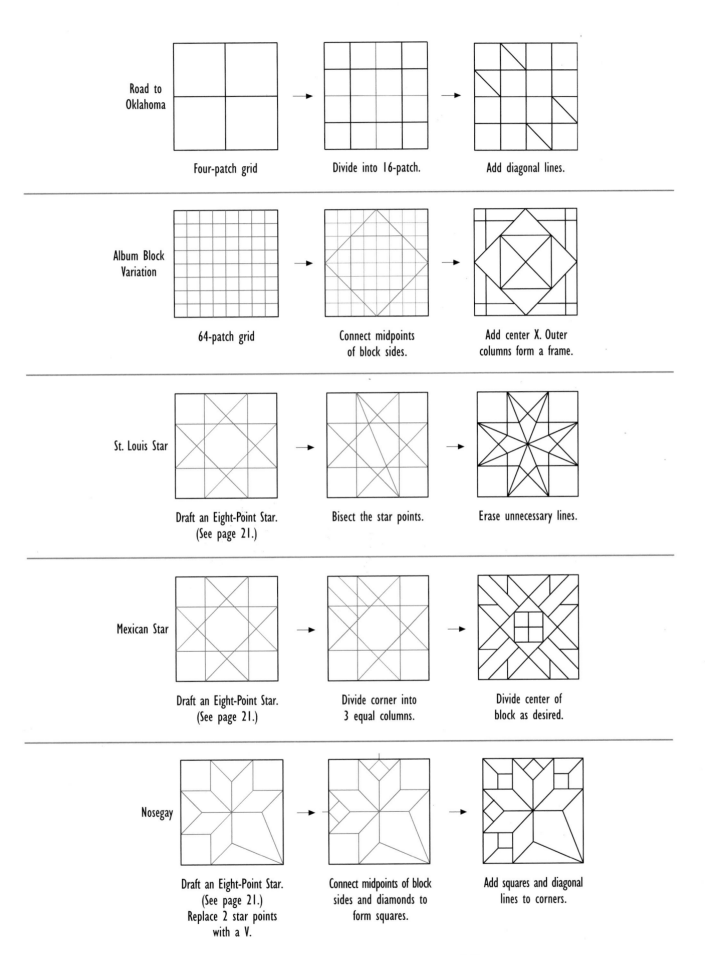

Road to Oklahoma

Four-patch grid → Divide into 16-patch. → Add diagonal lines.

Album Block Variation

64-patch grid → Connect midpoints of block sides. → Add center X. Outer columns form a frame.

St. Louis Star

Draft an Eight-Point Star. (See page 21.) → Bisect the star points. → Erase unnecessary lines.

Mexican Star

Draft an Eight-Point Star. (See page 21.) → Divide corner into 3 equal columns. → Divide center of block as desired.

Nosegay

Draft an Eight-Point Star. (See page 21.) Replace 2 star points with a V. → Connect midpoints of block sides and diamonds to form squares. → Add squares and diagonal lines to corners.

Hexagon or Midpoint Hexagon

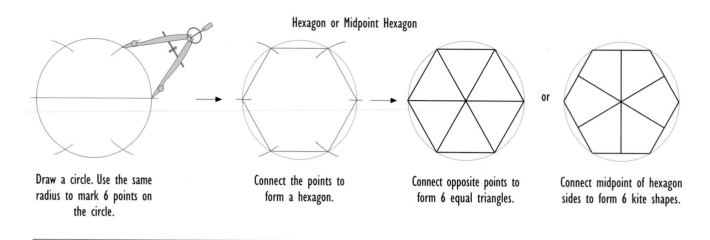

Draw a circle. Use the same radius to mark 6 points on the circle.

Connect the points to form a hexagon.

Connect opposite points to form 6 equal triangles.

or

Connect midpoint of hexagon sides to form 6 kite shapes.

Six-Point Star

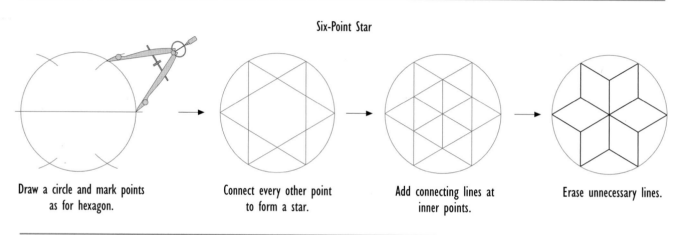

Draw a circle and mark points as for hexagon.

Connect every other point to form a star.

Add connecting lines at inner points.

Erase unnecessary lines.

Spinning Star by Jinny Beyer

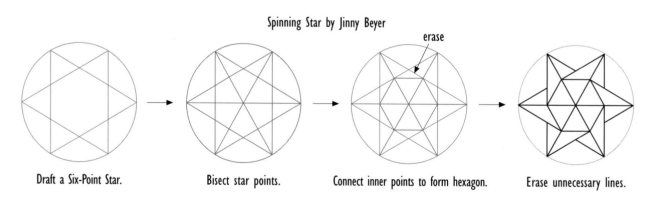

erase

Draft a Six-Point Star.

Bisect star points.

Connect inner points to form hexagon.

Erase unnecessary lines.

Fan Block

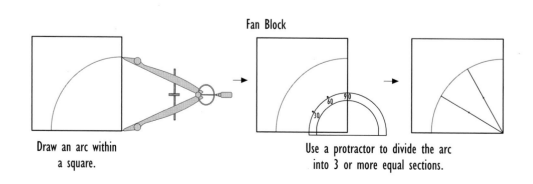

Draw an arc within a square.

Use a protractor to divide the arc into 3 or more equal sections.

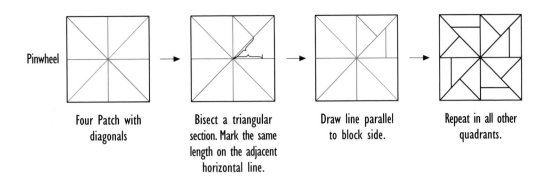

Pinwheel

Four Patch with diagonals → Bisect a triangular section. Mark the same length on the adjacent horizontal line. → Draw line parallel to block side. → Repeat in all other quadrants.

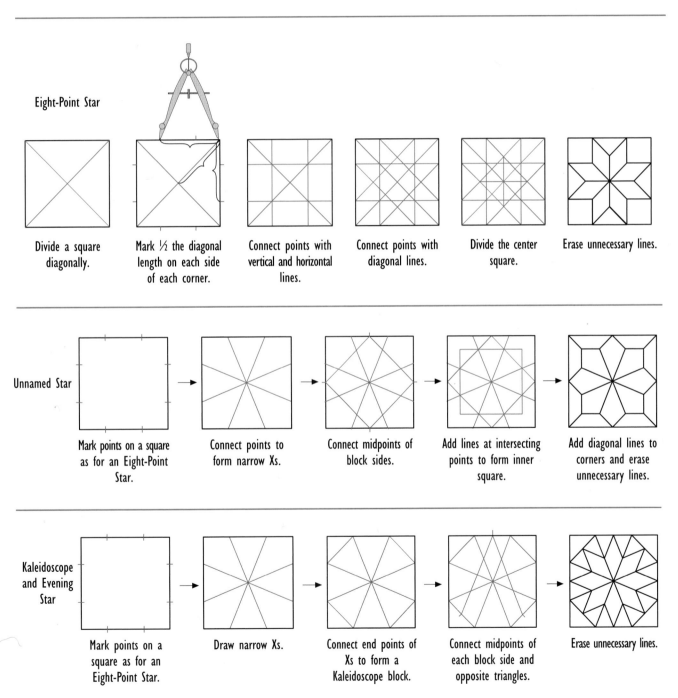

Eight-Point Star

Divide a square diagonally. → Mark ½ the diagonal length on each side of each corner. → Connect points with vertical and horizontal lines. → Connect points with diagonal lines. → Divide the center square. → Erase unnecessary lines.

Unnamed Star

Mark points on a square as for an Eight-Point Star. → Connect points to form narrow Xs. → Connect midpoints of block sides. → Add lines at intersecting points to form inner square. → Add diagonal lines to corners and erase unnecessary lines.

Kaleidoscope and Evening Star

Mark points on a square as for an Eight-Point Star. → Draw narrow Xs. → Connect end points of Xs to form a Kaleidoscope block. → Connect midpoints of each block side and opposite triangles. → Erase unnecessary lines.

To make a template, trace the exact pattern shape onto plastic.

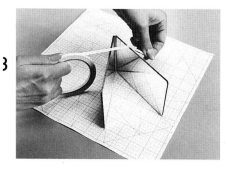

Add an accurate ¼"-wide seam allowance to all sides.

Open mirrors to match the angle of the pattern piece. Secure with tape across the top.

General Instructions

Making Templates

Once you have an accurate block pattern of the desired size, make an accurate template for your mirrored shape and for any other shape in the block that you cannot rotary cut.

Use translucent template plastic without grid lines. The plastic should not be thin and flimsy, or so thick or opaque that you cannot easily see the outlines of your print fabric through it. Make sure you can mark on it with a pencil. If the only plastic you can find is resistant to pencil markings, get a fine-tip marker that can be removed with a damp cloth. Don't use a permanent marker, because you will need to erase your markings and make new ones for each block.

1. Place the template plastic on top of the full-size pattern piece, leaving room to add seam allowances. Trace the exact shape of the finished piece onto the plastic (fig. 1).
2. Move the plastic onto a plain white sheet of paper. Then, using a thin, accurate, see-through ruler, add ¼" to each side of the finished shape for seam allowances (fig. 2).
3. Cut out the template exactly on this new line, not outside of it. Accuracy now will pay off later.

Securing the Angle of the Mirrors

Place your mirrors on top of the drafted pattern piece, with the hinge at the center of the star, pinwheel, or other shape, and the bottom edges along the sides (actual seam lines). Carefully place a piece of tape (¼"-wide masking tape works well) across the top of the mirrors, securing them at this angle (fig. 3).

Turn the mirrors upside down and place a short piece of tape on the sticky, open underside of the tape. This will keep the tape from sticking to itself when the mirrors are closed. Turn the mirrors right side up again. The mirrors are set to the correct angle for your design. You can pick them up and move them around easily.

Placing the Mirrors and Cutting

Open your fabric and lay it flat, in a single layer, on your cutting table. Place your mirrors on the fabric, open and secured to the correct angle for the block design you are using. Before you do any cutting, experiment by moving the mirrors around to various parts of the print to find the most interesting shapes and designs. Try placing the mirrors on odd parts of the motifs, as well as centering the motifs.

To see exactly how much of the print will be included in your design, use the template. If one side of the template plastic is easier to mark with a pencil, make this the top side. Pick up the template and notice where the actual sewing lines intersect at what will be the center of the rotating design. Take a large, fat needle and pierce a hole from the back side through the plastic at this intersecting point. (Later, you will use the hole to mark a dot at this seam intersection to make your piecing more accurate.) The pierced hole causes a little ridge on the surface of the plastic. Slip the template under the mirrors until the mirrors "snug up" against the ridge. The mirrors should be sitting right on the sewing lines marked on your template, and you should have an accurate idea of how much of the print will show in each pattern piece (fig. 4).

Once you have found an intriguing design with the mirrors and have slid the template under them to see exactly how much of the print will be captured in your template shape, analyze it a bit. Are there certain bold elements that you should try to line up along the sides? To make a big, asymmetrical leaf look more symmetrical, for example, position the mirrors and template so that the same amount will be showing on each side and the color "connects" from one piece to the next. Again, don't be fooled by the mirror image. The shapes may appear to connect in the mirror image, when in fact, they will not.

Measure along each side of the seam line on the template, from the center puncture point, and mark some reference points (at 1", 1¼", 1½", for example), to make sure the motif hits at the same point on each side. If you have a stripe in your fabric that would form an octagon in an eight-point center, it would certainly look better to have it match where pieces meet than to be a little bit off (figs. 5, 6).

When you need to center a motif vertically, draw a line down the center of your template (fig. 7). But don't feel that everything needs to be centered and symmetrical. All six or eight segments of a star must be cut in a consistent manner, but they may look great off-center.

When you have decided on the placement of the template, trace onto the plastic some of the dominant lines of the print under it. Don't trace every detail, just enough to recognize the shape so you can place the template exactly over the same motif elsewhere in the fabric. Include some reference points at each end of your template.

Sometimes, due to slight inaccuracies in cutting or piecing, a bit of bright color may appear in some pieces of a mirror-print design and not in others. This may be unavoidable, due to slight variations in the print. If you can "correct" an annoying spot with a good fabric marking pen, I won't tell!

Motifs may be close together, so that when you cut out a shape, you also cut into a neighboring motif. This is usually not a problem, since that same bit of print appears in all the rotating pieces and will just be part of

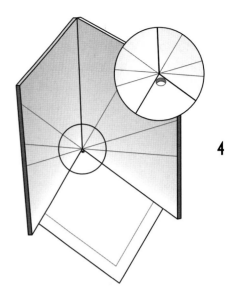

4

5

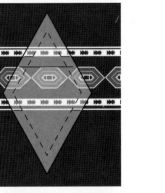

6

7

the design. However, if you really wanted to use the neighboring motif and now you can't because it is missing a chunk, you must make choices. It is wise to experiment and cut your favorite motifs first.

If you really want to plan and analyze your choices, cut several template shapes out of tracing paper. Work with a section of your fabric that contains one of each motif. When you find a design you like, pin one of the tracing-paper shapes in place on the print. Search for other designs, each time pinning a tracing-paper shape in place of the template. When you are done, some of the shapes may overlap and "cut" into each other. You can then choose between the two, move the design slightly so they don't overlap, or see if you have enough fabric to cut out the appropriate numbers of both designs. Using tracing-paper markers also comes in handy after

you have cut out so many pieces that your fabric won't hold together and you have a hard time counting repeats. Just pin a tracing-paper template to each one as you search your disjointed fabric for identical motifs.

Before you start cutting, be sure you have enough repeats of each motif for your design. If some of them lie near the edge of the fabric (top, bottom, or selvage edge), make sure the template isn't going to extend over the edge. If it does, you may need to change the placement slightly in order to have enough repeats for a given design.

If you have fairly thick template plastic and are adept at rotary cutting, you may be able to cut directly around the edge of the template itself. I find that a small rotary cutter is easier to maneuver than a large one for this. To prevent your template from slipping while cutting in this manner, let your

fingers hang off the back edge of the template, touching the fabric as you rotary cut (fig. 8), or try gluing a few small dots of sandpaper to the back side of the template—but not at the points.

If you prefer, or if you can't avoid slicing into your template, you can mark around the template with a pencil, then cut the shape out carefully with scissors or rotary cutter, cutting away the drawn line as you go. To keep the fabric from creeping as you trace around the template, slide a sheet of fine-grit sandpaper under your fabric.

Be careful not to overcut at the corners of the pieces. You will not be able to use an adjoining motif if you've sliced into it. After cutting, place the template over the cut piece to make sure it was cut the exact size of the template.

A Word about Grain Line

Because you have been searching out interesting designs and cutting out pieces any which way to achieve these designs, you have completely ignored grain line. Consequently, most of your mirrored-design shapes have bias edges. Train yourself to handle these pieces gingerly so you will not stretch them out of shape. Some slight stretchiness comes in handy as you try to match patterns from one piece to the next, but you do want your blocks to be straight and even.

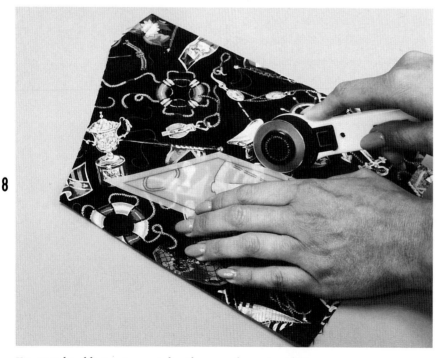

8

You may be able to rotary cut directly around your template.

If you cut and stitch accurately but still have problems, it may be due to bias edges stretching. If you mark and carefully match the seam-intersection points, stretched edges will be apparent and can be eased back in where needed. Sewing a bias edge to a straight-grain edge helps stabilize it. Stitch with the straight-grain piece on top and the bias piece on the bottom to control distortion. And finger-press rather than using an iron.

One of the easiest ways to ensure square blocks is to cut background pieces so that the edges that lie along the perimeter of the block are on the straight of grain.

It is usually easy to place the straight of grain along the outside edges of the block, because often the background pieces can be rotary cut. Most squares, rectangles, and half-square triangles don't require templates. Just measure the finished sides of your shape (from your drafted pattern) and add seam allowances.

Many odd-shaped background pieces also can be rotary cut. Make a template, adding seam allowances before you cut it out. Remembering that you want the straight of grain along the outside of the block, measure the width of the template (including seam allowances) and cut a strip of background fabric that wide. Open the strip, place the template on it, and cut along the edges (figs. 9, 10).

To cut more than one layer of fabric at a time, be sure all the strips are right side up. If you want the reverse shape in the same fabric, place one strip right side up and one right side down, or fold a single strip in half.

If you are working with a directional print or trying to center part of a print, make a template and cut your pieces individually, rather than rotary cutting them.

>·>·> NOTE <·<·<

Always determine whether the piece you are cutting can or should also be cut in the reverse. Be careful with asymmetrical shapes and print fabric. Cut a few pieces and lay out a block on your design wall to make sure you are cutting correctly.

>·>·> · <·<·<

Sewing Accurate Seams

No matter how painstakingly accurate you've been up to this point, if you sew a sloppy seam, you will cause yourself nothing but headaches. So take a moment before you begin piecing to be sure you have an accurate ¼" seam guide on your machine. I prefer not to use the edge of my presser foot, even if it is an accurate ¼", because I can't really keep an eye on the edge of the fabric if it is under the foot. I bring my needle down on the ¼" line on an accurate ruler, graph paper, or gridded template plastic; and place a piece of narrow masking tape on my machine. Then I can line up the edge of the fabric along the tape (fig.11).

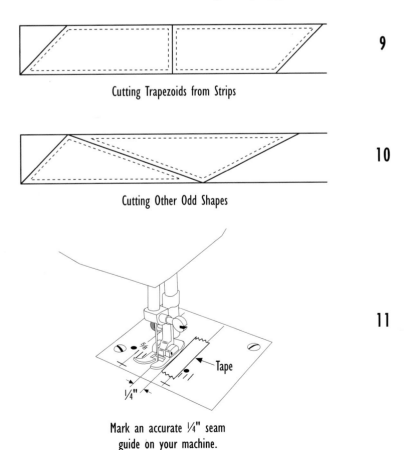

9

Cutting Trapezoids from Strips

10

Cutting Other Odd Shapes

11

Mark an accurate ¼" seam
guide on your machine.

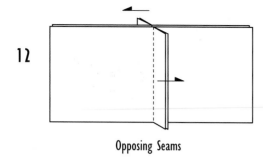

12

Opposing Seams

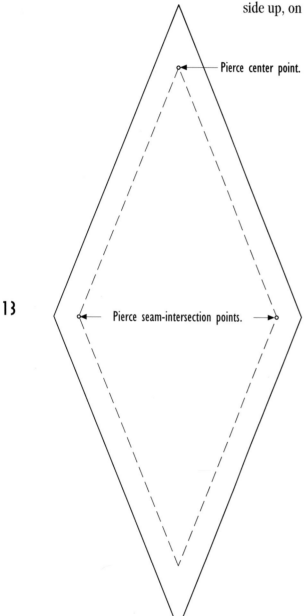

13

Pierce center point.

Pierce seam-intersection points.

Diamond Template for Eight-Point Star

Pressing

I prefer to finger-press rather than iron my blocks as I construct them, because so many pieces have bias edges that can easily be stretched out of shape by an iron. To finger-press, lay the two joined pieces, right side up, on a hard surface, such as your sewing-machine table. With the seam allowance laid toward the correct side, scrape your thumbnail backwards along the seam line to crease it. Be sure you are not forming a little tuck.

All-cotton fabrics will hold this crease until the block is finished. By then, there are usually background pieces with the straight of grain along the outside of the block to add stability. When the block is completed, press it from the right side, on top of a towel. The thickness of the seams sinks into the nap of the towel, so you get a nice flat surface. You can also make sure you are not forming small tucks along the seams or pressing the block out of shape. I use a dry iron for pressing during construction, then I use steam in the final pressing of the finished block to get it nice and flat.

When seams come together, it helps to distribute bulk and match seams if the top seam is pressed one direction and the bottom seam is pressed the other way. These are called opposing seams (fig. 12).

Piecing Eight-Point Stars and Centers

On your template, you marked the seam lines and pierced the center seam intersection with a fat needle. Pierce the plastic template also at the intersecting seam lines where a piece will be set in. The diamond template will have three small holes at the intersections of the seam lines (fig. 13).

A sharp pencil point should fit into these holes so that you can mark these points on the back side of your fabric pieces after you cut them out.

1. Place 2 diamonds right sides together. Using extra-fine pins, pin the center dots together and pin the outer dots together (fig. 14). If there are any important design lines in the print, be sure these also match.

> ·>·> **NOTE** <·<·<

Stitch from the points that will meet at the center of the star toward the outer edge. The center is the most important place for pieces to match. Sewing towards the center sometimes causes extra fabric to be eased in that direction, which results in distortion. If your machine tends to push the top fabric forward slightly as you are sewing, use a heavy pin or a seam ripper to push back on the top fabric with gentle strokes.

> ·>·> · <·<·<

2. Sew together the first 2 diamonds, starting at the edge of the fabric. Stop at the outer seam-intersection point and backstitch (fig. 15).

3. Finger-press the seam to one side. Construct 4 pairs of diamonds in this manner, pressing all seams in a counterclockwise direction.

4. Place 2 pairs, right sides together. Pin through the center seam intersection point on the top pair and through the same point on the bottom pair. Push the seam allowances out of the way, slide the 2 layers under the needle, and lower the needle until it is just above the pin.

Carefully remove the pin and lower the needle into the pin hole. Take 2 stitches forward, carefully take the same 2 stitches backward to secure the seam (or move your stitch length to "0" and take a few stitches in place), then sew forward, stopping at the outside dot and backstitching again. Repeat for the other half of the block (fig. 16).

5. Press this seam in the same direction as the others.

6. Place the halves right sides together. The seams should nestle together nicely. Set your stitch length to a longer stitch (about 8 stitches per inch) and take 5 or 6 stitches across the center. Open the halves to see if they match at the center of your block. If they do not match properly, the large stitches can easily be pulled out and you can try again for a perfect match without having to rip out an entire seam (fig. 17).

7. If the seams match, return your stitch length to normal (12 to 15 stitches per inch) and sew the center seam from one seam intersection point to the other.

8. To press the center seam, open the block and press so that the seams radiate in a counterclockwise direction. Press the right half of the center seam up and the left half down. The seam will separate in the center to form a little pinwheel (fig. 18).

Kaleidoscopes, pinwheels, and other eight-point center blocks that do not have set-in pieces are constructed in the same way as Eight-Point Stars except that you stitch to the outside edges of the pieces, rather than stopping at the seam-intersection points.

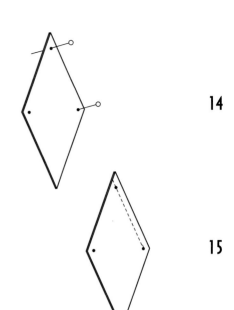

14

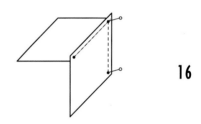

15

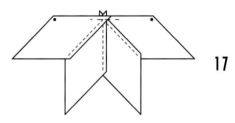

16

When sewing two sets of pairs together,
leave center ¼" unsewn;
push seam allowance out of the way.

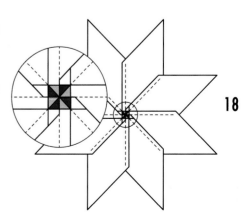

17

Take a few large test stitches through center,
check for accuracy, then sew dot to dot.

18

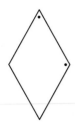

19

On Six-Point Stars, sew all seams
dot to dot, leaving center unsewn.

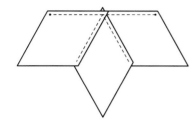

20

After testing center seam for accuracy,
sew the two halves together dot to dot.

21

Leave last ¼" of seams open
to accommodate set-in pieces.

22

23

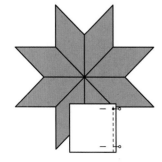

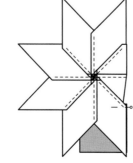
24

Piecing Six-Point Stars and Hexagons

1. To piece a Six-Point Star, sew the first 2 diamonds dot to dot, leaving the inner and outer ¼" unsewn, and securing stitches at each end. Press to one side (fig. 19).

2. Add a third diamond in the same way, matching seam intersections and pushing the seam allowances out of the way. Secure the stitches at each seam intersection. Press in the same direction as before.

3. Place the halves right sides together; match the center seams, following instructions for eight-point centers above; and stitch the halves together (fig. 20). Press seams so they radiate as for the Eight-Point Star blocks.

Piece hexagons in the same manner as Six-Point Stars, but sew from the center seam intersection all the way to the outside edges of each piece.

Stitching Set-in Pieces

Set-in pieces require accuracy—in cutting and stitching. Construct the center shape first (such as an Eight-Point Star). Leave the last ¼" of the seam, where pieces will be set in, unsewn with stitches secured (fig. 21). Be sure the seam-intersection point on the set-in piece is marked with a dot (fig. 22). I always work from the inside of a set-in piece to the outside edge.

1. With right sides together and the set-in piece on top, pin the seam-intersection points for the star and the set-in piece together. Place the inner pinned corner under the presser foot and lower the needle until it is just above the pinhole. Remove the pin carefully and lower the needle into the pinhole. Secure the stitches, then stitch to the edge of the fabric (fig. 23).

2. Turn the work so that the adjacent diamond is on top and the square on the bottom. Before stitching, slip your finger under the excess star fabric and slide it up and out of the way, forming a fold as shown (fig. 24). This prevents the fabric from getting caught in the seam and creates just the right positioning for the next seam. Match and pin seam-intersection points.

3. Secure the stitches at the seam intersection and sew to the outside edge. Set in other shapes in the same manner.

Sewing Curved Seams

The trick to sewing curved seams smoothly is putting the fullness where it belongs. Transfer matching points from the drafted pattern to your cut pieces (fig. 25). Pin matching points together, adjusting fullness evenly, and stitch with the convex piece on top.

Adding Borders

Before adding the borders to the quilt, be sure to measure, measure, measure! You need to know the dimensions of your top—not only what they should be, but what they are. Measure through the center of the quilt top horizontally and vertically. Then measure the outside edges. Are they larger? A small amount of difference can be eased in when you apply the borders. However, if the edges are significantly larger, perhaps you can adjust some seams to correct the problem so that your quilts' borders lie flat and straight.

To add straight borders:

1. Measure the length of the quilt top across the center. Cut 2 border strips to that measurement and sew them to the sides of the quilt top.
2. Measure the quilt top across the center, including the side borders. Cut 2 border strips to that measurement and sew them to the top and bottom of the quilt top (fig. 26).

To add mitered borders:

1. Estimate the finished outside dimensions of your quilt, including the borders. Cut border strips to this length and width plus at least ½" for seam allowances; add 2" to 3" to be safe.

> ·>·> **NOTE** <·<·<

If your quilt requires multiple borders, sew the strips together lengthwise and miter as a single border strip for greater ease and accuracy.

·>·> · <·<·<

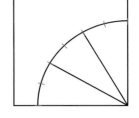

25

Mark several matching points on the drafted pattern, then transfer them to the fabric pieces.

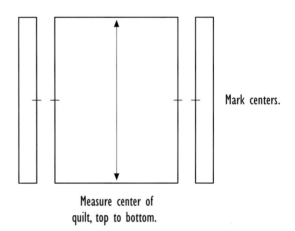

Mark centers.

Measure center of quilt, top to bottom.

26

Measure center of quilt, side to side, including borders.

Mark centers.

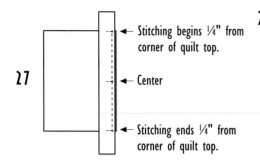

Stitching begins ¼" from corner of quilt top.

Center

Stitching ends ¼" from corner of quilt top.

27

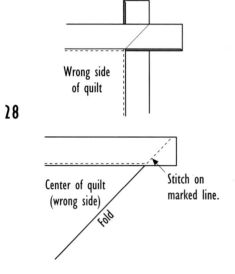

Wrong side of quilt

28

Center of quilt (wrong side)

Fold

Stitch on marked line.

2. Mark the centers of the quilt edges and the centers and end points of the border strips. Stitch the borders to the quilt with a ¼"-wide seam, matching the centers and end points. The border strip should extend the same distance at each end of the quilt. Start and stop your stitching ¼" from the corners of the quilt; press the seams toward the borders (fig. 27).

3. Lay the quilt on a table, wrong side up, with one border perpendicular to and overlapping the other. Mark a line from the corner of the quilt top to the outside edge of the border. Reverse the strips and mark the other border in the same way.

4. Fold the corner of the quilt diagonally to bring the border strips together. Match the lines, pin, and stitch along the marked line. (fig. 28).

5. Press the seam open and trim away excess fabric, leaving a ¼"-wide seam allowance.

6. Repeat with remaining corners.

Finishing Your Quilt

Before layering your quilt top for quilting, press it carefully. Trim the threads or triangular "tails" that might show through or create added bulk at the seams. Trim dark seams shorter than the light ones if they are shadowing through the top.

Piece backings so that the lengthwise grain runs vertically, especially for quilts that will hang on the wall, because the lengthwise grain has less stretch to it. Trim selvages, sew lengthwise pieces together, and press seams to one side. When layering the backing, batting, and top, make the backing and batting a couple of inches larger than the top on all sides.

To baste, secure the backing rather tautly to your table with spring clamps and/or masking tape, matching the centers of the backing and the table. Center the batting and the top. For hand quilting, baste the quilt in a grid, working from the center out. For machine quilting, pin-baste with safety pins.

Choosing a Quilting Design

If your quilt was designed by manipulating large-scale prints into beautiful swirling designs, you may feel, as I often do, that the real impact of the quilt is in the color and design and that a lot of detailed quilting is not necessary.

Evaluate each quilt to decide whether detailed quilting will enhance the design or be lost in it. The pattern you've chosen may have large expanses of plain background fabric, or your setting may contain plain alternate blocks that would benefit from a wonderful quilting design.

For most of my mirror-design quilts, I simply quilt to accent the new shapes formed by my print designs, then do some simple background quilting as needed. But if you have some plain spaces in which to show off some quilting, you may enjoy the section "Creating Your Own Quilting Designs," using mirrors, on page 86.

Binding

After quilting and before binding, check the quilt again. Is there any distortion? Are the sides straight and smooth? Measure through the center again and compare this measurement with the edges. Baste around the quilt, a scant ¼" from the edges. If the edges have stretched slightly, you can draw up this thread to correct the problem. Use a long ruler and a rotary cutter to trim the batting and backing, making sure the edges are as straight and even as possible, and square in the corners.

I prefer a ½"-wide, double-fold binding. The width of the seam allowance should be the same as the width of the binding. If the top design only leaves a ¼"-wide seam allowance, trim the batting and backing ¼" wider than the top for a ½"-wide binding.

1. Cut the binding strips 6 times wider than the finished width, plus a little extra—about ¼" for a low-loft batting. For ½" binding, cut strips ½" x 6 = 3" + ¼" = 3¼". Cut these strips on the crosswise grain unless you have curved edges on your quilt or just prefer a bias binding. Sew strips together, end to end, with diagonal seams to distribute bulk (fig. 29). Trim seams to ¼" and press open. The length of this continuous strip should be the perimeter of your quilt, plus about 9".

2. Trim one end at an accurate 45° angle and press under ¼". Fold the strip in half lengthwise, right sides out, and press (fig. 30).

3. Leaving a tail of binding at least 4" or 5" long, begin stitching the binding to the quilt at least 6" away from a corner, aligning the raw edges of the binding with the raw edges of the quilt. Stitch to ½" (or binding width, if different) from the corner of the quilt. Stop and backstitch (fig. 31).

4. Remove the quilt from under the needle. Turn it counterclockwise and fold the binding up, so that it forms a diagonal fold at the corner (fig. 32).

5. Fold the binding down so that the raw edges of the binding align with the next side of the quilt to be sewn (fig. 33).

6. Begin stitching ½" (or binding width) from the corner, securing stitches. Do not catch the fold in the stitching. Complete all four corners in this manner.

7. Trim the ending tail and tuck it inside the beginning tail, or mark the joining points and sew the ends together by machine with a diagonal seam (fig. 34).

8. Fold the binding over to the back of the quilt and blindstitch in place. It should just cover the row of machine stitching on the back side.

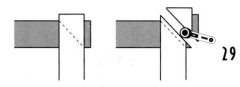

29

Sew binding strips together with a diagonal seam.

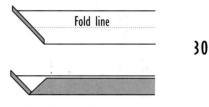

30

Fold strip in half lengthwise; turn under beginning ¼".

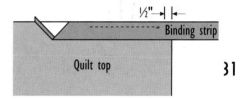

31

Stop stitching ½" from end for ½" binding. Backstitch.

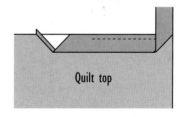

32

Fold binding strip up, forming a diagonal fold.

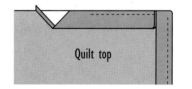

33

Fold strip down, aligning edges.

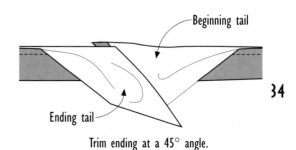

34

Trim ending at a 45° angle.

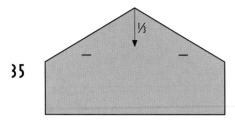

35

Make two buttonholes in pocket piece.

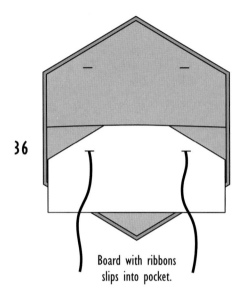

36

Board with ribbons slips into pocket.

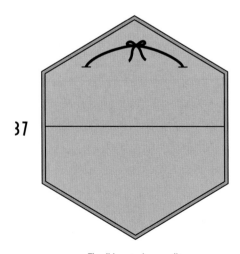

37

Tie ribbon to hang quilt.

At the corners, the miter should form a diagonal fold on the top and back sides. To distribute bulk, make sure the fold goes to one side on the front and toward the opposite side on the back of each corner. As you hand stitch the binding to the quilt, pass the needle to the front at the corner and take a couple of blind stitches on the mitered fold. Pass the needle to the back and take a couple blind stitches on the back miter fold, then continue.

Hanging an Odd-Shaped Quilt

Several years ago, *Quilter's Newsletter Magazine* published some tips on hanging odd-shaped quilts (November/December 1989). I used their ideas to successfully hang all of my round quilts. The method works well with hexagonal quilts and other shapes that won't accommodate the usual hanging sleeve.

The basic idea is to put a pocket on the back on the quilt to hold a foam-core board the same shape as the upper half of the quilt. This board, which is like two thin layers of posterboard with a ¼" layer of styrofoam between them, supports the points or other odd shapes of the quilt. Add the pocket after the quilt is quilted but before the binding is applied.

1. Measure the width of the quilt and the distance from the center to the top. Cut the pocket fabric a couple of inches larger in both directions.

2. Turn the bottom edge under ¼", press, turn under again, and stitch.

3. Measure from this edge, which runs across the center back of your quilt, to where the top point of your quilt will be. Then measure from the top back toward the center a little less than one-third of the distance. At this height, stitch 2 widely spaced ¼"-long buttonholes (fig. 35). Pierce the buttonholes.

4. Lay the pocket, right side down, on a table and position the quilt over it, right side up. Be sure the hemmed edge of the pocket runs across the middle of the quilt, with the raw edges sticking out above. Baste the pocket and quilt together and trim.

5. Apply the binding through all layers.

6. Lay the top half of the quilt on a piece of foam-core board, with the lower edge of the pocket along the edge of the board. Trace around the top edge of the quilt, then remove it. Draw another line, just inside the first, depending on the width of your binding. (For ½"-wide binding, draw the line ½" inside the first line.)

7. Cut the foam core to this size with a craft knife. Slip the foam core into the pocket. Mark dots on the foam-core board through the two buttonholes and remove the board.

8. Pierce small holes at the dots to match up with the buttonholes. Thread a ribbon through the holes in the board (fig. 36).

9. Slide the board into the pocket and thread the two ends of the ribbon through the buttonholes in the pocket. Tie the two ends of the ribbon together, just below the edge of the quilt, and hang the quilt by a single nail or hook (fig. 37).

Gallery of Quilts

⇧ *City Slicker Stars* by Gail Valentine, 1995, Austin, Texas, 63" x 87". *Cross-legged cowboys and bucking broncs are among the intriguing Eight-Point Star designs, while cowboy boots form the centers of the Mexican Star blocks.*

⇧ **Spinning Star Galaxy** *by Gail Valentine, 1995, Austin, Texas, 53" x 32". The Spinning Star block was designed by Jinny Beyer in 1979. Here, the mirror-print blocks interlace in a challenging asymmetrical setting.*

⇩ **Three Stars** *by Lorraine Mossman, 1995, Leander, Texas, 20½" x 44". Lorraine used a multicolored floral paisley fabric to create subtle but elegant swirling stars, separated by a Mexican Star block.*

⇧ *Floral Kaleidoscope* by Gail Valentine, 1995, Austin, Texas, 90¼" x 109". *Two fabrics (same print, different-colored background) compose the mirrored blocks that alternate with solid blocks to form an illusion of circles. The queen-size quilt is framed with a dogtooth border.*

Reflections on a Christmas Morn ⇨
by Ann Byrd, 1995, Austin, Texas, 50"
diameter. Ann wanted a tree skirt, so she
adapted Hearthsewn's "Christmas Stars"
pattern, substituting her mirrored Six-
Point Star blocks for the Feathered Star
blocks. She used a Christmas floral and
quilted with a walking foot to avoid
stretching the gold Sliver™ thread.

Christmas Flowers by Jill Bacon, ⇨
1995, Austin, Texas, 30" x 30". Jill used
the St. Louis block, Evening Star, the
Eight-Point Star, and the Unnamed Star,
alternating with the Mexican Star for a
wonderful Christmas (or anytime!) wall
hanging. Jill used fabric with the same
print as Ann Byrd's, but in a different
color. What a contrast!

⇦ **Nosegay** by Gail Valentine, 1995, Austin, Texas, 45 ½" x 45 ½". Quilted by Patty Cline. A stunning tropical floral print was the basis for this vibrantly colored quilt. A unique mirrored quilting design, inspired by the floral print, is used in the corners.

Christmas by Stars and Candlelight by Kathleen H. ⇨ McCrady, 1995, Austin, Texas, 32" x 32". Using a Kaleidoscope variation and the Mexican Star, Kathleen repeats a pleasing plaid theme throughout the quilt. Notice how her color placement makes one shape merge into another.

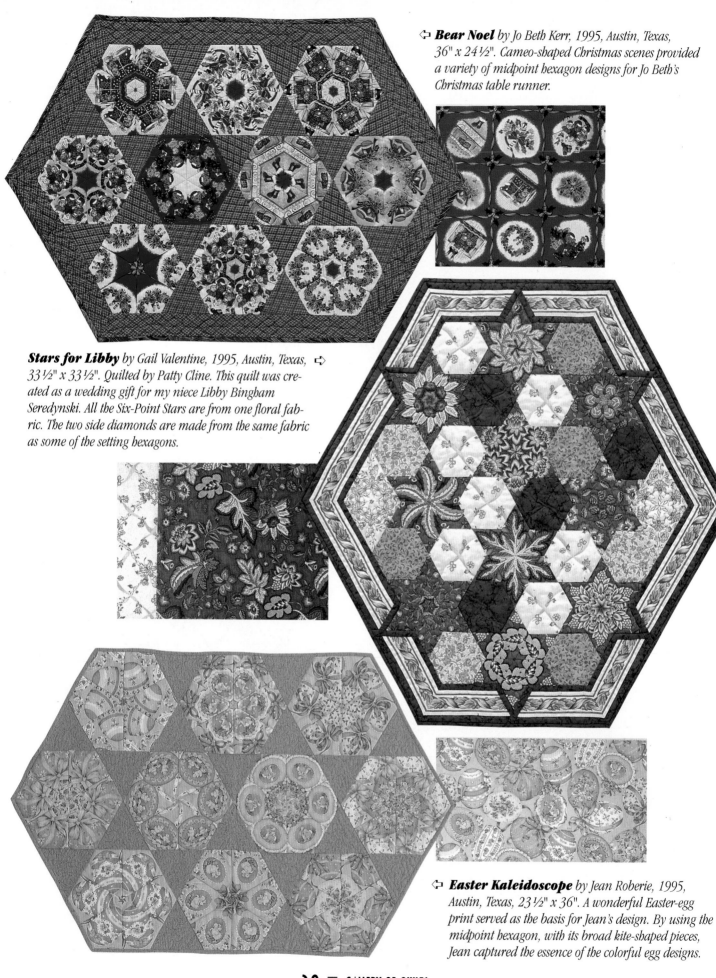

Bear Noel by Jo Beth Kerr, 1995, Austin, Texas, 36" x 24½". Cameo-shaped Christmas scenes provided a variety of midpoint hexagon designs for Jo Beth's Christmas table runner.

Stars for Libby by Gail Valentine, 1995, Austin, Texas, 33½" x 33½". Quilted by Patty Cline. This quilt was created as a wedding gift for my niece Libby Bingham Seredynski. All the Six-Point Stars are from one floral fabric. The two side diamonds are made from the same fabric as some of the setting hexagons.

Easter Kaleidoscope by Jean Roberie, 1995, Austin, Texas, 23½" x 36". A wonderful Easter-egg print served as the basis for Jean's design. By using the midpoint hexagon, with its broad kite-shaped pieces, Jean captured the essence of the colorful egg designs.

↢ **Tropical Twist** by Gail Valentine, 1995, Austin, Texas, 30½" x 26½". A bright and bold tropical-fish print creates intriguing designs in this simple midpoint hexagon design.

Challenge Star by Gail Valentine, 1991, Bountiful, ⇨ Utah, 42" x 36". A large paisley and two striped prints make up the Six-Point Star blocks. One of the striped prints also works well for the border.

↢ **Primarily Bears** by Melinda Noonan, 1995, Cedar Park, Texas, 38½" x 33". Melinda used the Six-Point Star block, then expanded each one into a framed hexagon. The setting triangles form a central star design.

Balloon Ballistics *by Marcia Kaylakie,* ⇨
*1995, Austin, Texas, 37 ½" x 37 ½". Marcia
felt challenged by the St. Louis Star design but
succeeded in combining a wonderful hot-air-
balloon print with vibrant colors for a daz-
zling quilt.*

⇦**One Piece at a Time** *by Joanie
Weeden, 1995, Austin, Texas,
57" x 57". Joanie used a great
Southwest print for the Evening Star
block, and near solids for the
Pinwheel blocks. She played very
successfully with color and design
lines and introduced additional
motifs in the pieced border.*

Flying Swallows by Gail Valentine, 1995, Austin, Texas, 32 ¾" x 32 ¾". A single, large, bordered block serves as a charming wall hanging. Its smaller pieces make this design suitable for medium-scale prints.

Playful Pinwheels by Gail Valentine, 1995. Austin, Texas, 52 ¾" x 52 ¾". Fanciful critters in biplanes and parachutes swirl in the easy Pinwheel blocks. An explosion of color is perfect for a juvenile quilt.

Tutti-frutti by Lisa Braun Kushwara, 1995, ⇨
Austin, Texas, 30" x 41". A dramatic print in unusual
colors sets the tone for Lisa's unique midpoint hexagon
quilt, which she hand quilted beautifully.

⇦ *Viva Senorita* by Joan Pratt, 1995, Austin, Texas,
30½" x 42". Joan used a colorful Southwest print for
her Unnamed Star blocks and had great fun discovering
the hidden designs. The print border was the perfect
complement.

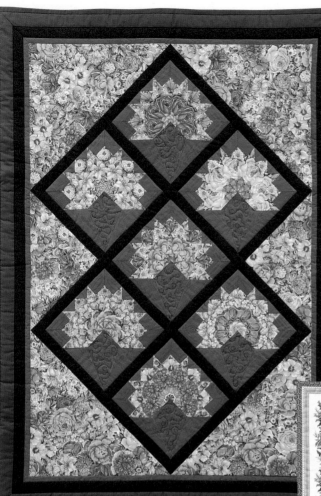

⇦ **Window Trellis** by Mary Raper, 1995, Austin, Texas, 42" x 58". Mary found myriad designs in this colorful floral fabric, which she also used in the corners of her quilt. Mary added nonadjacent mirror-print repeats between the pieces of the central mirrored design for a blooming effect.

Fans by Gail Valentine, 1995, Austin, Texas, 36½" x ⇨ 50½". Quilted by Mary Raper. Light- and dark-background versions of the same print create the mirrored fan designs. Relatively simple cutting and piecing make this a fast, fun quilt.

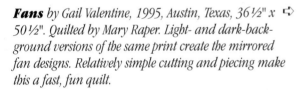

St. Louis Star *by Gail Valentine, 1995, Austin, Texas,* ⇨
*37" x 52". Quilted by Mary Raper. An unusual jewel-tone
Southwest print is abstracted into colorful swirling stars.
Large outer star points allow for even more color.*

⇦ **Fancatsic** *by Phyllis O'Rourke, 1995, Austin, Texas,
29" x 37". Phyllis used the Fan block and a playful cat
fabric to create this whimsical wall hanging. All of her
cat-loving friends want one like it.*

⇦**A Summer Day for Doris** by Erika A. Rogala, 1995, Austin, Texas, 41½" x 41½". Erika combined the Unnamed Star and Pinwheel blocks with a fanciful floral/fruit-and-vegetable print for a terrific quilt made to bring a little Texas sunshine to a friend in Germany. A radiating quilting design enhances the overall effect.

St. Louis Star Cherubs by Rebecca L. Salinger, 1995, ⇨ Austin, Texas, 43" x 59". Cherub panel motifs form the centers of the stars in this striking quilt, and the sashing strips form gold crosses.

Rod 'n' Reel by Gail Valentine, ⇨
1995, Austin, Texas, 48" x 48".
Fish, fishermen, and fishing gear
swirl into fantastic designs in the
Unnamed Star blocks. The two-tone
background and pieced border
combine for added dimension.

⇦ *Road to Oklahoma by Gail Valentine,*
1995, Austin, Texas, 30" x 30". Two different
Southwest prints combine for some interesting
visual effects in this simple Four Patch design.
A band of bright color on the inner border
makes the quilt sparkle.

⇧ **Tea Time** *by Gail Valentine, 1995, Austin, Texas, 59½" x 59½". Reminiscent of the '30s, this traditional-looking quilt makes great use of a teapot print in a variation of the Album block. A border repeating the on-point squares adds a real zing to the quilt.*

Projects and Patterns

Using the Patterns

Each pattern is prefaced with fabric suggestions and helpful notes. Start with a small, simple project for your first attempt at this technique. Once you've actually worked with the mirrors, it's much easier to understand the exciting things you can do with them.

Patterns are provided on the following pages for 10 of the quilts pictured in the gallery. They are meant to serve as guidelines if you want to create a similar quilt. Chances are that you will not find the same fabric and duplicate the quilt exactly, but you may find a similar *type* of print to substitute. Think of the pieced blocks, alternate blocks, and sashing or setting units in these quilt plans as building blocks to use any way you like for a design that pleases you.

Yardages were calculated based on 42 usable inches of fabric width. Crosswise strips in the cutting are based on that width. A 2"-wide strip is listed as 2" x 42"—do not trim it if your strip is slightly wider. In the cutting charts, the letter "r" next to a template letter indicates the template must be reversed to cut those pieces. If you prefer lengthwise-grain borders (I do for wide strips), refigure those yardage amounts. I wait to measure and cut borders until my quilt top is completed. All bindings were calculated for ½"-wide French double-fold binding, cut 3¼" wide.

Customize Your Quilt!

The following quilts were designed to work with the prints that were used. The sizes of the blocks, along with the sizes and colors of the borders and sashings, were chosen to work with the prints. The prints you choose may require different sizes of blocks and other elements. I hope that you will feel free to make changes as you go along. If you like the block design but don't want to tackle the pieced border that's shown, simply substitute a plain border—or no border at all. If you wish to redraft any of the blocks to another size, see "Adjusting Scale: Drafting" on page 18. Trust your own inclinations in color and design. After all, it's your quilt and it should please you. Have fun, and Happy Quilting!

Fans

The Fan block is fairly easy to piece and only requires three pattern repeats. In this quilt, light and dark versions of the same print alternate in the two center Fan blocks in each row. If you don't have both light and dark versions of the same print, just use six repeats of one color.

Arrange the fans any way you want. See "Fancatsic" on page 44 and the diagonal-setting illustration on page 17 for more ideas. Here, I wanted to achieve a strippy effect, arranging the fans in horizontal rows with sashing in between. In order to clearly delineate the fans, some of which contained a light fabric against a light background, I outlined the central fans with narrow braid.

◆ Finished Quilt Size: 36½" x 50½" ◆ Finished Block Size: 7", 5½" fan radius ◆ Color photo on page 43. ◆

Materials: 44"-wide fabric

Theme print: 3 repeats for corner fans; 6 repeats
for central fans.
Optional: 3 light and 3 dark repeats of the same
printed motif or 6 repeats of one fabric.
¾ yd. for background
⅜ yd. for sashing*
1⅝ yds. print for border**
1⅝ yds. for backing

⅝ yd. for binding
2¾ yds. braid to outline central fans (optional)

* The directional print used in the sample required sashing
cut on the lengthwise grain. If this is the case with your
fabric, buy ⅞ yd. A total of 1 yd. is enough to make both
sashing and binding.

** Buy this amount if the border print contains 4 repeats of
the desired stripe or design. Buy more if the border print
requires centering to match corner motifs or if the printed
motif you choose is wider.

Cutting

Use Templates A and B on page 89. Mark matching points from the templates on the backs of the fabric pieces.

Fabric	FIRST CUT No. of Pieces	Dimensions	ADDITIONAL CUTS No. of Pieces	Dimensions	No. of Triangles
Theme print	60 Template A *15 light motifs and 45 dark motifs*				
Background	20 Template B				
Sashing	4 strips	2¼" x 28½"			
Border	2 strips	4¾" x 41" *cut on the lengthwise grain*			
	2 strips	4¾" x 54" *cut on the lengthwise grain*			

> ·>·> **TIP** <·<·<

To cut the background pieces, cut 3 strips,
7½" x 42", and from the strips, cut 20 Template
B as shown.

> ·>·> · <·<·<

Piecing the Blocks

For two-tone center fans, one block will contain fan
blades in a dark-light-dark sequence, and the adjoining
block will contain blades in a light-dark-light sequence.

1. Sew 3 fan blades (piece A) together, stitching from the
wide edge to the center, matching design elements of
the print if necessary.

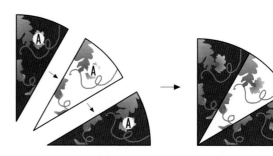

2. With right sides together and the background piece (piece B) on top, pin the fan and background pieces together at the matching points and the ends, distributing the fullness evenly between the pins.

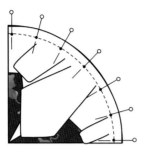

With right sides together,
pin matching points.

3. Place the work flat on the sewing machine with the background piece up. Sew from one edge to the other, occasionally lifting the presser foot, with the needle down, and readjusting the fabric to prevent tucks.

4. Press the seam toward the darker fabric.

Assembling and Finishing the Quilt Top

1. Arrange the fans in rows of 4 across as shown and sew them together.

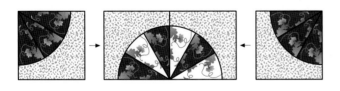

2. Attach braid if desired.

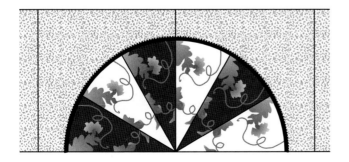

3. Sew the sashing strips to the rows of fans, making sure the block seams are properly aligned.

4. Referring to "Adding Borders" (mitered) on page 29, center border strips at the sides and the top and bottom of the quilt top; measure and mark the desired end points.

5. Stitch border strips to the edges of the quilt, beginning and ending ¼" from corners (secure stitches). Miter the corners.

6. Layer the quilt top with batting and backing. Baste, quilt, bind, and label your quilt.

Tea Time

This Album Block Variation is fairly simple to piece. By placing different colors in opposite corners of the blocks, you can create a four-patch unit at the block intersections and an interesting secondary design. My print contained sixteen different designs. If yours does not, try using some of the same designs upside down for different looks.

This block is especially suitable for an old-fashioned or traditional look with softer colors. It works best with symmetrical motifs. The inner border is a spacer strip to make fitting the pieced border easy.

◆ Finished Quilt Size: 59½" x 59½" ◆ Finished Block Size: 12" ◆ Color photo on page 47 ◆

Materials: 44"-wide fabric

Theme print: 4 repeats for each block,
    16 different motifs or variations
1¼ yds. green (¾ yd. for large triangles and ½
    yd. for border)
½ yd. pink for small triangles and squares
1⅛ yds. coral (½ yd. for small triangles and
    squares, and ⅝ yd. for border)

1 yd. yellow solid (⅝ yd. for blocks and ⅜ yd.
    for border)
1 yd. yellow print #1 (⅝ yd. for blocks and ⅜ yd.
    for border)
1 yd. yellow print #2 (⅜ yd. for spacer strips and
    ⅝ yd. for binding)
3¾ yds. for backing

Cutting
Use Templates A and B on page 91.

Fabric	FIRST CUT No. of Pieces	Dimensions	ADDITIONAL CUTS No. of Pieces	Dimensions	No. of Triangles
Theme print	64 Template A *4 repeats for each of 16 blocks*				
Green	4 strips	5⅛" x 42"	32 squares	5⅛" x 5⅛"	64 △
	5 strips	2" x 42"	104 squares	2" x 2"	
Pink	1 strip	5½" x 42"	8 squares *cut 1 from scraps*	5½" x 5½"	32 ⊠
	2 strips	2" x 42"	32 squares	2" x 2"	
Coral	1 strip	5½" x 42"	8 squares *cut 1 from scraps*	5½" x 5½"	32 ⊠
	2 strips	2" x 42"	32 squares	2" x 2"	
	4 strips	3⅜" x 42"	50 squares *cut 2 from scraps*	3⅜" x 3⅜"	200 ⊠
Yellow solid	4 strips	2" x 42"	32 Template B and 32 Br		
	2 strips	3½" x 42"	26 squares *cut 2 from scraps*	3½" x 3½"	

2" ↕ | B \ B | B \ B | B \ B |

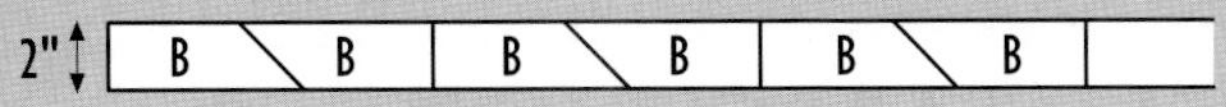

Stack 2 strips right side up, 2 right side down.

Yellow print #1	4 strips	2" x 42"	32 B and 32 Br		
	2 strips	3½" x 42"	26 squares *cut 2 from scraps*	3½" x 3½"	
Yellow print #2	5 strips	2" x 42"*			

*Wait to cut these strips until the pieced border is completed in case adjustments are necessary.

Piecing the Blocks

1. Join 4 theme-print triangles to form the center square.

2. Sew a large green triangle to each side.

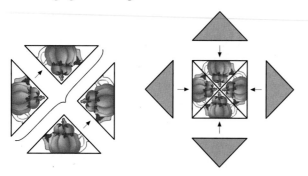

3. Sew a yellow solid B to a small pink square, and a pink triangle to a yellow solid Br. Press seams toward the pink and sew the units together.

4. Sew a yellow print #1 B to a small coral square, and a yellow print #2 Br to a coral triangle. Press toward the coral.

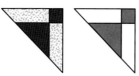

Make 2 of each color combination per block.

5. Sew corner units to the block as shown.

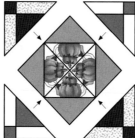

6. Join the blocks into rows, 4 across and 4 down, and sew the rows together.

Adding Borders and Finishing

1. Add a small coral triangle to each side of a small green square as shown, to form a triangle unit.

Make 96.

2. Sew triangle units to the sides of the yellow solid and print squares as shown. Make 10 units per side, plus 4 left end units and 4 right end units. Notice that the yellow solid and print squares alternate along the border.

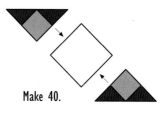

Make 40.

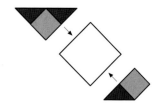

Left End Unit
Make 2 with yellow solid and 2 with yellow print #1.

Right End Unit
Make 2 with yellow solid and 2 with yellow print #1.

3. Sew the border units together in diagonal rows.

4. Measure the completed border strips and the finished quilt top across the center. The quilt should finish 48" x 48", and borders should finish 51" long, allowing for a 1½" spacer strip on each side. Cut spacer strips 2" wide, or adjust as necessary if the measurements of your quilt and/or borders are different.

5. Sew the spacer strips together end to end. Cut 2 strips, each 48½" long, and sew them to the sides of the quilt top. Cut 2 strips, each 51½" long, and sew them to the top and bottom.

6. Add the pieced border strips, beginning and ending the stitching ¼" from the corners (secure stitches).

7. Join the 2 small green squares at each end, stitching from the corner outward.

8. Construct corner units as shown and stitch to the corners.

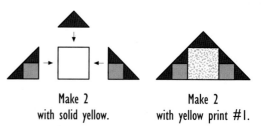

Make 2 with solid yellow.

Make 2 with yellow print #1.

9. Layer the quilt with batting and backing. Baste, quilt, bind, and label your quilt.

Road to Oklahoma

The Road to Oklahoma is easy to draft and piece, and it only requires four repeats. The challenge is to create a mirrored design that flows from one segment to the next and doesn't look off-balance. I used two different prints in this quilt, but you need not fill all the squares with mirrored-print motifs.

This design would also make a great sixteen-block quilt, with dark fabric in the centers of the Xs, and light-print motifs forming four-patch designs in four places, between the quadrants of the quilt.

◆ Finished Quilt Size: 30" x 30" ◆ Finished Block Size: 12" ◆ Color photo on page 46 ◆

■ 55

Materials: 44"-wide fabric

Theme prints: 1 print with a light background and 1 with a dark background, 4 repeats for each block

½ yd. light background for blocks

⅝ yd. navy blue (⅓ yd. for blocks and ⅓ yd. for outer border)

⅓ yd. gold for inner border

1 yd. for backing

½ yd. for binding

Cutting

Use Template A on page 57.

| Fabric | FIRST CUT | | ADDITIONAL CUTS | | |
	No. of Pieces	Dimensions	No. of Pieces	Dimensions	No. of Triangles
Dark-background theme print	16 Template A *4 repeats for each of 4 squares*				
Light-background theme print	12 Template A *4 repeats for center square 2 repeats of each of the 4 other "side" motifs*				
Light background	1 strip	3½" x 42"	16 squares *cut 4 from scraps*	3½" x 3½"	
	1 strip	3⅞" x 42"	8 squares	3⅞" x 3⅞"	16 ◻
Navy blue	2 strips	2½" x 26½"			
	2 strips	2½" x 30½"			
	1 strip	3⅞" x 42"	8 squares	3⅞" x 3⅞"	16 ◻
	4 squares	3½" x 3½" *cut from scraps*			
Gold	2 strips	1½" x 24½"			
	2 strips	1½" x 26½"			

Piecing the Blocks

1. Join each light triangle to a dark triangle, to form a square. Press seam toward the darker fabric.

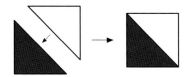

2. Arrange the pieces of each block on your design wall as shown. Arrange adjacent blocks so that they have a mirror-image orientation of light and dark pieces, forming the **X**-shaped design and the mirror-print designs at the center and at the side edges of the quilt top.

3. Sew the pieces together into rows of 4. Sew the rows together to form the blocks, pressing the seams in opposite directions from row to row.

4. Sew the 4 blocks together, carefully matching the center motif in each.

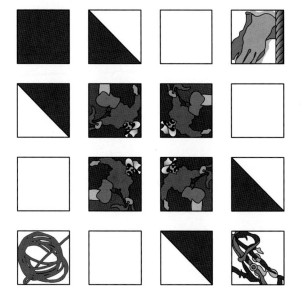

Adding Borders and Finishing

1. Sew the 24½"-long gold inner border strips to the sides, then the 26½"-long strips to the top and bottom.

2. Add the 26½"-long navy blue outer border strips to the sides, then the 30½"-long strips to the top and bottom.

3. Layer the quilt with batting and backing. Baste, quilt, bind, and label your quilt.

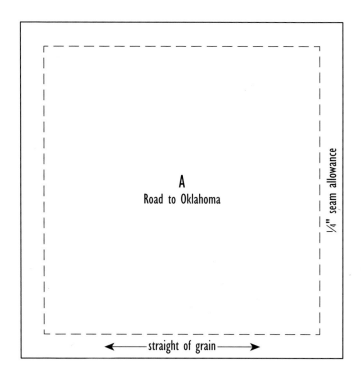

A
Road to Oklahoma

¼" seam allowance

← straight of grain →

Tropical Twist

This simple little quilt can look quite dramatic. The block is made of six identical pieces. The equilateral setting triangles join the blocks in rows. Look for other quilts using this block in the Gallery of Quilts on pages 33–47. Build a longer or wider quilt, depending on how many blocks you want to make, or square off the shape by adding corner shapes as in "Tutti-frutti" on page 42. This block works particularly well with large motifs, since the kite shape is fairly broad at one end.

◆ Finished Quilt Size: 30½" x 26½" ◆ Color photo on page 39 ◆

Materials: 44"-wide fabric

Theme print: at least 6 repeats for each of
  7 blocks
¼ yd. for setting triangles

1 yd. for backing
½ yd. for hanging pocket (optional)
⅜ yd. binding

Cutting

Use Templates A and B on page 90.

| Fabric | FIRST CUT | | ADDITIONAL CUTS | | |
	No. of Pieces	Dimensions	No. of Pieces	Dimensions	No. of Triangles
Theme print	42 Template A *6 repeats for each of 7 blocks*				
Background	1 strip	5⅛" x 42"	12 Template B		

5⅛"

Piecing the Blocks

Refer to "Piecing Six-Point Stars and Hexagons" on
page 28.

1. Sew 3 Template A kite
   shapes together, leav-
   ing the center ¼"
   unsewn.
2. Repeat with the other
   3 Template A.
3. Sew the center seam
   from edge to edge.

Assembling and Finishing the Quilt Top

1. Arrange the blocks in rows of 2, 3, and 2 blocks, with
   the flat side along the top and bottom of each block.
   Arrange 12 setting triangles between and around the
   outside of the blocks to form a large hexagon.
2. Add triangles to the blocks as shown to form diagonal
   rows; sew the rows together.

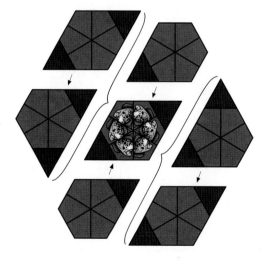

3. Layer the quilt top with batting and backing. Baste,
   quilt, bind, and label your quilt.

>·>·> TIP <·<·<

*If you choose to hang the quilt with the point at the
top, you may wish to make a hanging pocket. See
"Hanging an Odd-Shaped Quilt" on page 32. Add the
pocket before binding.*

>·>·> · <·<·<

Challenge Star

This Six-Point Star design was made from a multicolored large paisley, a blue wallpaper stripe, and a red floral-striped border print. The stars are set in vertical rows, with just the tips touching, so that setting hexagons fit between them. The background edge fillers are the shapes formed when the edges are squared off to the tips of the outermost hexagons. For added interest, I divided three of the hexagons in the quilt into six curved triangles. The Six-Point Star is suitable for a wide variety of fabrics (See "Reflections on a Christmas Morn" on page 36 and "Primarily Bears" on page 39.)

◆ Finished Quilt Size: 42" x 36" ◆ Color photo on page 39 ◆

Materials: 44"-wide fabric

Theme prints: 2 or 3, 6 each of 19 repeats for star blocks

⅞ yd. of 1 or more fabrics for background and setting pieces

⅞ yd. to 1 yd. border stripe*

1⅓ yds. for backing

¾ yd. for hanging pocket (optional)

⅜ yd. for binding

* Choose a lengthwise stripe with 6 repeats across for the border. You may need extra to center the motifs so that mitered corners will all match. (See "Border Prints" on page 83.)

Cutting
Use Templates A, B, C, D, and E on pages 90–91.

Fabric	FIRST CUT		ADDITIONAL CUTS		
	No. of Pieces	Dimensions	No. of Pieces	Dimensions	No. of Triangles
Theme print	114 Template A *6 repeats for each of 19 different stars*				
Background	4 strips	4" x 42"	36 Template B*		
	3 strips	2⅝" x 42"	6 Template E		
			6 Template Er		
			6 Template D		

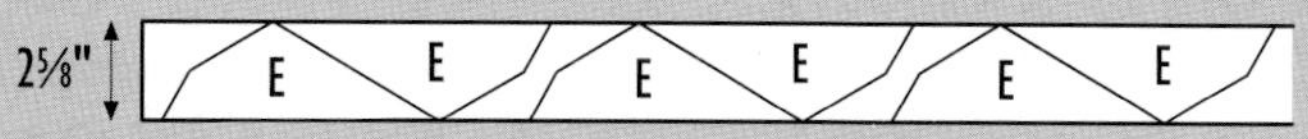

Place 2 strips right sides together.

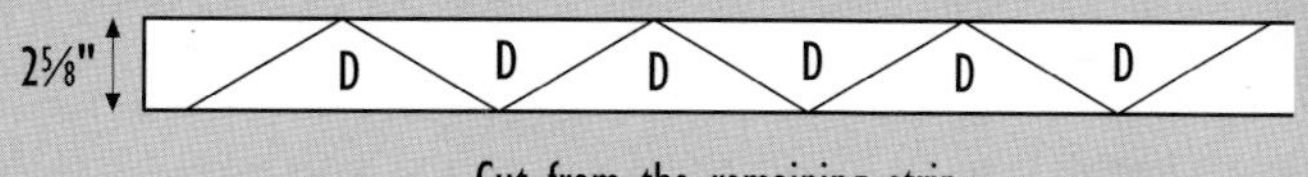

Cut from the remaining strip.

Border stripe	6 strips *Adjust for your border print*	2⅛" x 23"			

*Optional: For 3 curved-piece hexagons, cut 9 Template C from light fabrics and 9 from slightly darker fabrics.

Piecing the Blocks

Refer to "Piecing Six-Point Stars and Hexagons" on page 28.

1. For each mirror-print star, sew together 3 star points, leaving the inner and outer ¼"-wide seam allowances unsewn. Repeat with the remaining 3 star points.

Make 2.

2. Sew the star halves together, leaving the ¼"-wide seam allowances at the outer edges unsewn.

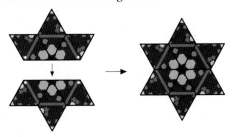

Assembling and Finishing the Quilt Top

1. Arrange the stars and background pieces on your design wall until you have a pleasing design.
2. Set in the background hexagons between the star points. (See "Stitching Set-in Pieces" on page 28.)

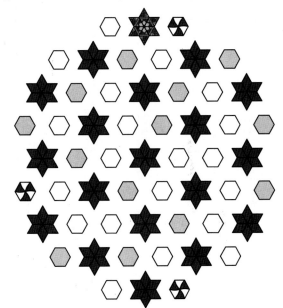

3. Set in the background pieces, E and E reversed, to form the 6 corners of the quilt. Join E and Er along their adjacent edges.
4. Set in the background piece D in the remaining edge spaces.

5. Measure the quilt top to be sure that all 6 sides are the same length (approximately 18½" plus seam allowances). Referring to "Adding Borders" (mitered) on page 29, center the border strips, with the same printed motif at the midpoint of each side.
6. Pin and sew border strips to the quilt top, beginning and ending the stitching ¼" from the corners (secure stitches). Miter each of the 6 corners at a 60° angle.
7. Layer the quilt top with batting and backing. Baste and quilt. Referring to "Hanging an Odd-Shaped Quilt" on page 32, construct a hanging pocket. Bind and label your quilt.

Nosegay

When I think of the Nosegay pattern, I think of charming 1930s pastel florals. But this vivid, tropical floral fabric suggested a different approach. The pattern is based on an Eight-Point-Star grid with 45° diamonds, but only six diamonds are used, requiring only six repeats. The block looks good set on point, which leaves empty corner triangles to fill. I designed a quilting motif using mirrors on the floral-print fabric. (See "Creating Your Own Quilting Designs" on page 86.) The "Window Trellis" quilt on page 43 also contains the Nosegay block.

◆ Finished Quilt Size: 45½" x 45½" ◆ Finished Block Size: 12" ◆ Color photo on page 37 ◆

Materials: 44"-wide fabric

Theme print: at least 6 repeats of 4 different motifs
1⅜ yds. aqua for background
¼ yd. pink for small squares
¼ yd. teal for cones

⅝ yd. for sashing and outer border
¼ yd. for inner border
2¾ yds. for backing
⅝ yd. for binding

Cutting

Use Templates A, B, C, and D on pages 92–93.

| Fabric | FIRST CUT | | ADDITIONAL CUTS | | |
	No. of Pieces	Dimensions	No. of Pieces	Dimensions	No. of Triangles
Theme print	24 Template A *6 repeats for each of 4 blocks*				
Aqua	2 squares	22⅛" x 22⅛"			4 ◻
	4 squares	3¾" x 3¾" square			16 ⊠
	2 strips	2¼" x 44" *cut on the lengthwise grain*	12 Template D 12 Template Dr		

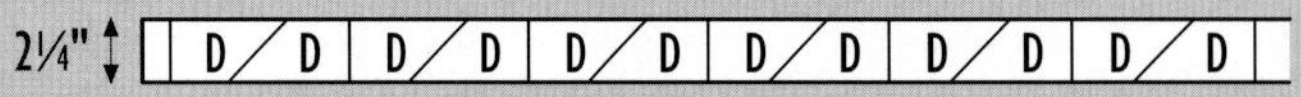

2¼" ↕ | D⁄ D⁄ D⁄ D⁄ D⁄ D⁄ D⁄ D⁄ D⁄ D⁄ D⁄ D |

Place 2 strips right sides together.

| | 2 strips | 3" x 25" *cut on the lengthwise grain* | 4 Template C 4 Template Cr | | |

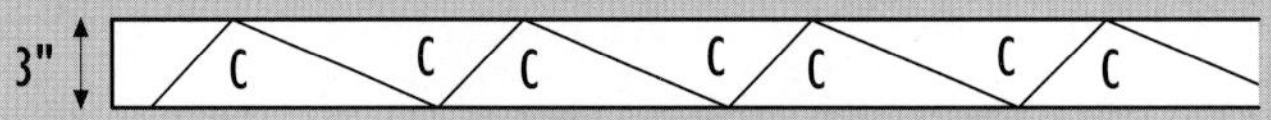

3" ↕ | ⁄C C⁄ C ⁄C C⁄ C ⁄C C |

Place 2 strips right sides together.

Pink	1 strip	2¼" x 42"	20 squares *cut 2 from scraps*	2¼" x 2¼"	
Teal	4 Template B				
Sashing and outer border	3 strips	2" x 26"			
	2 strips	2" x 29"			
	2 strips	2" x 12½"			
	2 strips	2" x 43"			
	2 strips	2" x 46" *piece necessary length from scraps*			
Inner border	2 strips	1¼" x 29"			
	2 strips	1¼" x 30½"			

Piecing the Blocks

Refer to "Piecing Eight-Point Stars and Centers" on page 26 and "Stitching Set-in Pieces" on page 28.

1. Sew a piece D trapezoid to a small square, stitching from the inner seam intersection to the outer edge.

2. Set in a piece Dr trapezoid to make the corner background unit.

   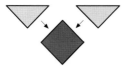

Make 3
for each block.

3. Sew 2 small aqua triangles to a small square to make the side background unit.

Make 2
for each block.

4. To construct the flower, sew the theme-print diamonds together in pairs, leaving the outer ¼"-wide seam allowances unsewn (secure stitches).

5. Join pairs, leaving the center and outer seam allowances unsewn.

6. Join 1 pair of diamonds to one side of the cone, and sew the other pairs of diamonds together, leaving center seam allowances unsewn. Press all seams counterclockwise.

7. Sew the 2 halves together, leaving outer seam allowances unsewn.

8. Set in a background unit between each star point as shown; set in oblong background pieces on either side of the cone.

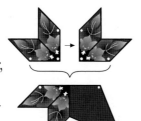

Assembling and Finishing the Quilt Top

1. Arrange blocks with 12½"-long sashing strips between them. Sew the blocks and sashing strips together.

2. Sew the 26"-long sashing strips to the blocks as shown.

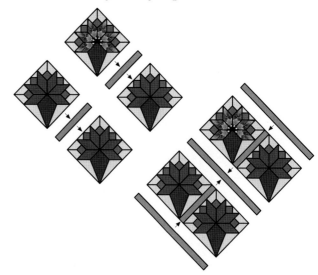

3. Sew the 29"-long sashing strips to the remaining 2 sides.

4. Sew the 29"-long narrow border strips to 2 sides, then sew the 30½"-long strips to the other sides.

5. Add the 4 corner background triangles.

6. Add the 43"-long border strips to 2 sides, then the 46"-long strips to the remaining sides.

7. Mark a quilting design on the quilt top. Layer the quilt top with batting and backing. Baste, quilt, bind, and label your quilt.

City Slicker Stars

Eight-Point Stars in a wonderful Southwest print team with the Mexican Star block for an interesting secondary design in this quilt. The four-patch center of the Mexican Star block accommodates another mirrored design, using a cowboy-boot print. From a distance, the design may look like a flower. Up close, you see it's a cowboy with a rope. It was great fun to make even the most asymmetrical motifs connect from one wedge to the next.

◆ Finished Quilt Size: 63" x 87" ◆ Finished Block Size: 12" ◆ Color photo on page 33 ◆

Materials: 44"-wide fabric

Theme prints: 1 or more prints with at least
    8 repeats for each of the 8 Eight-Point Star
    blocks and 1 smaller-scale print with at least
    4 repeats for each of the 7 Mexican Star blocks
1⅜ yds. light gold for background
⅜ yd. red for Mexican Star stripes
½ yd. blue for Mexican Star points

¾ yd. black (¼ yd. for surrounding motif in
    Mexican Star and ½ yd. for first border)
2⅛ yds. print (⅝ yd. for second border and
    1½ yds. for fourth border)
1 yd. gold for third border
5¼ yds. for backing
⅞ yd. for binding

Cutting

Use Templates A, B, C, and D on page 92.

Fabric	FIRST CUT		ADDITIONAL CUTS		
	No. of Pieces	Dimensions	No. of Pieces	Dimensions	No. of Triangles
Theme prints	64 Template A *8 repeats for each of 8 blocks* 28 Template B *4 repeats for each of 7 blocks*				
Light gold background	4 strips	4" x 42"	32 squares	4" x 4"	
	3 strips	6¼" x 42"	15 squares	6¼" x 6¼"	60 ⊠
	3 strips	3¼" x 42"	28 squares	3¼" x 3¼"	56 ◺
Red	5 strips	2⅛" x 42"	28 Template D		
Blue	6 strips	2⅛" x 42"	28 Template C		
			28 Template Cr		

2⅛" ↕ | C / C | C / C | C / C | C / C | C |

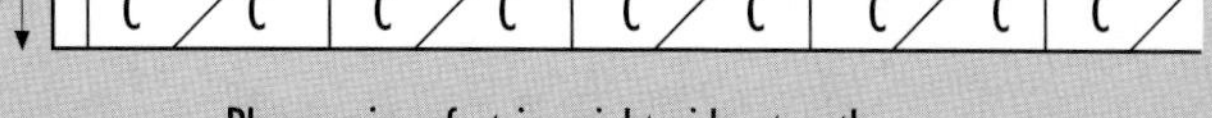

Place pairs of strips right sides together.

Fabric	FIRST CUT		ADDITIONAL CUTS		
Black for blocks and first border	1 strip	3⅜" x 42"	14 squares *cut 2 from scraps*	3⅜" x 3⅜"	28 ◺
	6 strips	2¼" x 42"			
Print for second and fourth borders	7 strips	2¾" x 42"			
	8 strips	6" x 42"			
Gold for third border	7 strips	4½" x 42"			

Piecing the Eight-Point Star Blocks

Refer to "Piecing Eight-Point Stars and Centers" on page 26.

1. Sew diamonds together in pairs, from the center edge to the outside seam intersection.

2. Sew pairs together, leaving the center and outer seam allowances unsewn and securing stitches.

3. Sew star halves together, leaving outer seam allowances unsewn. Press all seams counterclockwise.

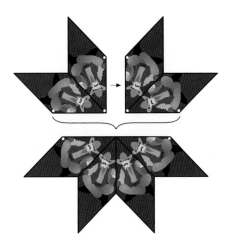

4. Set in squares at corners, and large triangles at sides, between star points. (See "Stitching Set-in Pieces" on page 28.)

Piecing the Mexican Star Blocks

1. Sew together 4 piece B, then add 4 small triangles to sides.

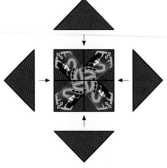

2. Sew small background triangles to blue pieces C and Cr.

3. Sew 1 of each of these units to the sides of the piece D trapezoids.

4. Add 2 of these units to the center square.

5. Join the block pieces in diagonal rows, adding the large background triangles to the ends of the top and bottom rows.

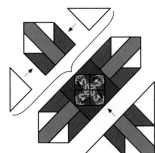

Assembling and Finishing the Quilt Top

1. Arrange the blocks in rows, 3 across and 5 down, alternating the 2 types of star blocks.

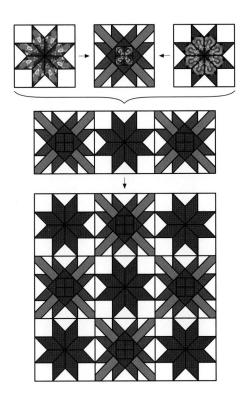

2. Sew the border strips of each color together end to end, then cut:

First Border (black)
2 strips, each 2¼" x 44"
2 strips, each 2¼" x 68"

Second Border (print)
2 strips, each 2¾" x 48½"
2 strips, each 2¾" x 72½"

Third Border (gold)
2 strips, each 4½" x 56½"
2 strips, each 4½" x 80½"

Fourth Border (print)
2 strips, 6" x 68½"
2 strips, 6" x 92½"

3. Referring to "Adding Borders" (mitered) on page 29, sew the border strips together lengthwise into units, then sew a border unit to each side of the quilt top, beginning and ending the stitching ¼" from the corners. Miter the corners.

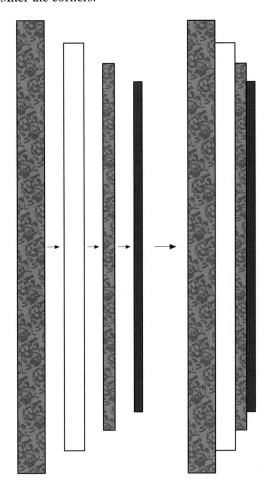

4. Layer the quilt top with batting and backing. Baste, quilt, bind, and label your quilt.

Playful Pinwheels

This pattern works wonderfully with juvenile prints. Try cartoon characters, playful animals, fairytale figures, spaceships—even dinosaurs! The background color in each block can be different (as pictured) or all the same. Although this block has an eight-point center, it is different from Eight-Point Star designs because the central shape rotates—the short side of one triangle joins to the long side of the next triangle. It works well with asymmetrical motifs, which "spin" and create interesting designs. The mirrors will help isolate interesting shapes and splashes of color, but asymmetrical designs do not give a true image of the finished design. Just focus on color and be willing to accept some great surprises.

◆ Finished Quilt Size: 52¾" x 52¾" ◆ Finished Block Size: 12" ◆ Color photo on page 41 ◆

Materials: 44"-wide fabric

Theme print: at least 8 repeats of 9 different motifs or variations

⅞ yd. for background*

⅞ yd. for sashing

½ yd. red for inner border

⅜ yd. blue for outer border

3⅜ yds. for backing

⅔ yd. for binding

* This is the amount you will need if you use the same background for all the blocks. If you want to use different-colored backgrounds, buy ¼ yd. for each block.

Cutting

Use Templates A and B on pages 91 and 95.

Fabric	FIRST CUT No. of Pieces	Dimensions	ADDITIONAL CUTS No. of Pieces	Dimensions	No. of Triangles
Theme print	72 Template A *8 repeats for each of 9 blocks*				
Background	6 strips	2¼" x 42"	36 Template B		
	2 strips*	7¼" x 42"	9 squares	7¼" x 7¼"	36 ⊠

> ·>·> **NOTE** <·<·<

If using different colors, cut one 7¼" square and cut twice diagonally to yield 4 triangles. Cut a strip from the remainders, 2¼" x 23½". From this strip, cut the 4 Template B trapezoids.

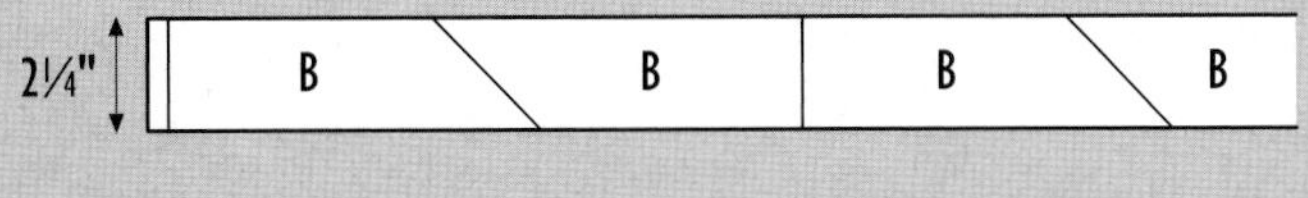

> ·>·> · <·<·<

2¼" | B / B | B / B |

Sashing	9 strips	3" x 42"	12 rectangles	3" x 12½"	
Red	5 strips	2⅝" x 42"			
Blue	6 strips	1¾" x 42"			

Piecing the Blocks

Refer to "Piecing Eight-Point Stars and Centers" on page 26.

1. Sew a print triangle to a background triangle. Press toward the darker fabric.

Make 4.

2. Sew a print triangle to a Template B trapezoid. Press toward the darker fabric.

Make 4.

3. Sew the units together to make a quarter-block by stitching along the diagonal seam, edge to edge, starting from the center. Press toward the trapezoid unit.

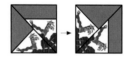

4. Sew 2 quarter blocks together, leaving the center seam allowance unsewn (secure stitches), and stitching to the outside edge. Press seams in a counterclockwise direction.

5. Sew the halves together, matching centers as for an Eight-Point Star, then stitching edge to edge. Press all center seams counterclockwise.

Assembling and Finishing the Quilt Top

1. Sew 5 sashing strips, each 3" x 42", end to end and cut into strips, each 46½" long.

2. Arrange the blocks in rows of 3 with the 12½" sashing pieces as shown. Sew the blocks and sashing pieces together into vertical rows. Sew the 46½"-long sashing strips between these rows and on both sides.

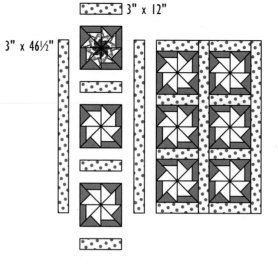

3" x 12"

3" x 46½"

3. Sew the red border strips end to end and cut 2 strips, each 46½" long, and 2 strips, each 50¾" long.

4. Sew the 46½"-long red border strips to the left and right sides of the quilt top. Sew the 50¾" red strips to the top and bottom.

5. Sew the blue border strips end to end and cut 2 strips, each 50¾" long, and 2 strips, each 54¾" long.

6. Sew the 50¾"-long blue border strips to the left and right sides of the quilt top. Sew the 54¾" blue strips to the top and bottom.

7. Layer the quilt top with batting and backing. Baste, quilt, bind, and label your quilt.

R od 'n'
R eel

This adaptable block contains eight equal kite-shaped pieces with a background "frame." In this quilt, I used a two-tone background similar to an Attic Windows block to give it a little more dimension. The same block appears in "Viva Senorita" on page 42,

and "A Summer Day for Doris" on page 45. If you decide to tackle the dramatic border, accuracy is essential to match all of the points.

◆ Finished Quilt Size: 48" x 48" ◆ Finished Block Size: 12" ◆ Color photo on page 46 ◆

Materials: 44"-wide fabric

Theme print: at least 8 repeats for each of
    9 blocks
½ yd. gold for background
1⅛ yds. navy blue for blocks and pieced border
    background

½ yd. light gold print for pieced border
1 yd. beige for pieced-border background
3⅛ yds. for backing
⅝ yd. for binding

Cutting
Use Templates A–K on pages 94–95.

Fabric	FIRST CUT No. of Pieces	Dimensions	ADDITIONAL CUTS No. of Pieces	Dimensions	No. of Triangles
Theme print	72 Template A *8 repeats for each of 9 blocks*				
Dark gold	5 strips	2¼" x 42"	36 Template B		
Navy blue	5 strips	2¼" x 42"	36 Template B		
	1 strip	3⅝" x 42"	4 Template C		
	6 strips	2" x 42"	24 Template D		
			24 Template Dr		
	1 strip	1⅞" x 42"	4 Template G		
			4 Template Gr		
		cut from scraps {	4 Template I		
			4 Template Ir		
Light gold print	6 strips	2" x 42"	24 Template D		
			24 Template Dr		
	1 strip	1⅝" x 42"	4 Template H		
			4 Template Hr		
Beige	8 strips	2⅛" x 42"	48 Template E		
			48 Template Er		
	4 strips	2⅜" x 42"	48 Template F		
			48 Template Fr		
	1 strip	2¼" x 42"	4 Template J		
			4 Template Jr		
		cut from scraps {	4 Template K		
			4 Template Kr		

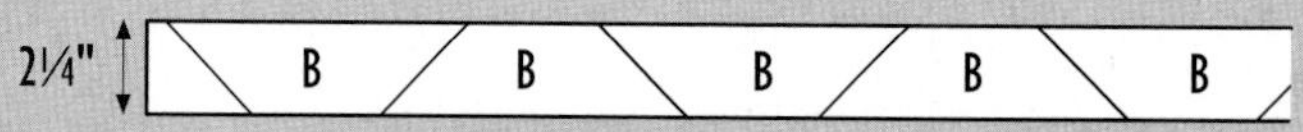

(Dark gold strip diagram: 2¼" strip showing B B B B B pieces cut diagonally)

Piecing the Blocks

Refer to "Piecing Eight-Point Stars and Centers" on page 26 and "Stitching Set-in Pieces" on page 28.

1. Sew the Template A star wedges together into pairs, leaving outer ¼"-wide seam allowances unsewn for set-in pieces. Finger-press to one side.

2. Sew pairs of wedges together into half stars, beginning and ending the stitching ¼" from the edges. Continue pressing in the same direction.

3. Machine-baste the center 1" of the halves together, check center seams for matching, then stitch from seam intersection to seam intersection. Press seams in the same direction.

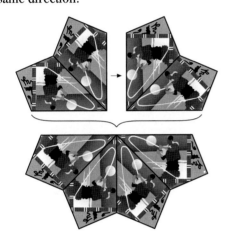

4. Set in the gold background pieces between the star points on half of the block. At the 4 corner star points, leave the ¼"-wide seam allowances unsewn, then sew the corner trapezoids to each other with a diagonal seam. Press seams toward the star.

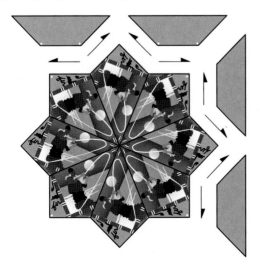

5. Set in the navy blue background pieces on the other half of the block.

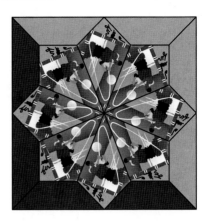

6. Arrange the blocks with background colors all in the same orientation and sew them together in 3 rows of 3. Press seams in opposite directions from row to row.

Piecing the Border and Finishing

Each border unit finishes 3" x 6". The two-tone units change direction at the center, on either side of the solid wedge (piece C) so that the dark halves face the center.

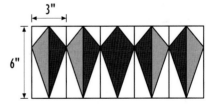

1. Sew together pieces D and Dr.

Make 24.   Make 24.

2. Add pieces F, Fr, E, and Er to the D/Dr and C units as shown.

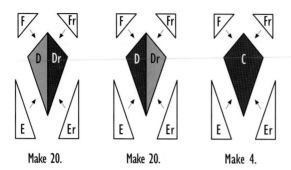

Make 20. Make 20. Make 4.

3. Construct the following border end and corner units:

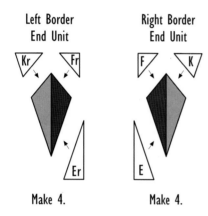

Left Border End Unit Right Border End Unit

Make 4. Make 4.

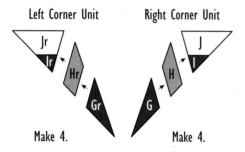

Left Corner Unit Right Corner Unit

Make 4. Make 4.

4. Add the border end and corner units to the border ends.

5. Measure the quilt top and border strips. Both should measure 36½" long. Sew the borders to the quilt top, matching center points, end points, midblock points, and seam intersections as shown in the photograph on page 73. Begin and end stitching ¼" from the corners.

6. Sew the border strips together at the diagonal corner seams. Press border seams toward the quilt top.

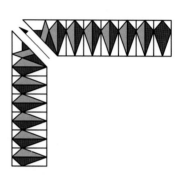

7. Layer the quilt top with batting and backing. Baste, quilt, bind, and label your quilt.

St. Louis Star

To capture as much of the mirrored-print effect as possible, I drafted the St. Louis Star as a 15" block. The two-tone outer star points frame and contain the mirrored designs, creating a dramatic impact of color. To avoid large blank spaces at the block intersections, I added a small four-point star design—a wedge pieced in the corner of the blocks. See also "Ballon Ballistics" on page 40 and "St. Louis Star Cherubs" on page 45.

◆ Finished Quilt Size: 37" x 52" ◆ Color photo on page 44 ◆

Materials: 44"-wide fabric

Theme print: at least 8 repeats of 6 motifs for stars

¼ yd. light and ¼ yd. dark in 3 colors (6 total) for outer star points

1 yd. for background

⅓ yd. for first border
¼ yd. for second border
½ yd. for third border
1¾ yds. for backing
⅝ yd. for binding

Cutting

Use Templates A, B, C, and D on page 96.

| | FIRST CUT | | ADDITIONAL CUTS | | |
Fabric	No. of Pieces	Dimensions	No. of Pieces	Dimensions	No. of Triangles
Theme print	48 Template A *8 repeats for each of 6 blocks*				
Light outer star-point colors	8 Template B for each block				
Dark outer star-point colors	8 Template Br for each block				
Background	3 strips	4⅞" x 42"	24 squares	4⅞" x 4⅞"	
	1 strip	7½" x 42"	6 squares *cut 1 from scraps*	7½" x 7½"	24 ⊠

>·>·> OPTIONAL PIECED CORNERS <·<·<

Instead of 8 of the 4⅞" background squares above, cut 8 Template C and 8 Template Cr. From 2 small print motifs, cut 4 repeats of each, using Template D.

First border	5 strips	1½" x 42"
Second border	5 strips	1" x 42"
Third border	5 strips	2½" x 42"

Piecing the Blocks

Piece this block in wedge-shaped units to avoid set-in pieces.

1. Sew a light star-point B to a background square, and a printed piece A to a dark star-point Br. Press toward the solid star points.

2. Join these segments, matching opposing seams.

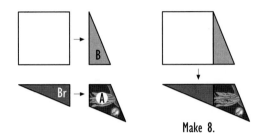

Make 8.

Optional Pieced Corners

1. Sew print piece D to background piece Cr, securing stitches but leaving seam allowances unsewn where piece C will be set in.

2. To set in piece C, stitch from the center dot out, in each direction. Use this unit in 1 corner of each of 4 stars, as you would the squares above.

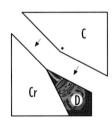

3. Sew a background triangle to a light star point, and a dark star point to a theme print A. Press toward the solid star points. Join these segments. Press toward the small theme-print star.

4. Join 2 wedges, stitching from outer edge to center edge. Carefully match star points at the outer ¼" seam line as shown. Press seams counterclockwise.

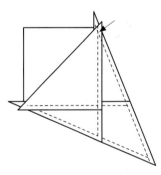

5. Sew pairs of wedges together, leaving the center seam allowance unsewn (secure stitches). Press counterclockwise.

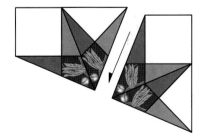

6. Sew the block halves together, first checking the center for matching seams, then stitching edge to edge. Press the tips of star points open at the outer edges of the block to distribute bulk.

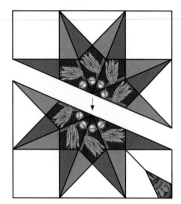

Assembling and Finishing the Quilt Top

1. Arrange the blocks in rows of 2 across and 3 down, orienting them to form the optional mirror-print corner designs. Sew them together into rows.

2. Sew the rows together.

3. Sew border strips together end to end and cut:

First Border
2 strips, each 1½" x 35½"
2 strips, each 1½" x 50½"

Second Border
2 strips, each 1" x 36½"
2 strips, each 1" x 51½"

Third Border
2 strips, each 2" x 41"
2 strips, each 2" x 56"

4. Sew the 3 strips for each side of the border together lengthwise, matching the center points of each strip. Sew to the quilt top as a single unit, beginning and ending the stitching ¼" from the corners. Miter the corners.

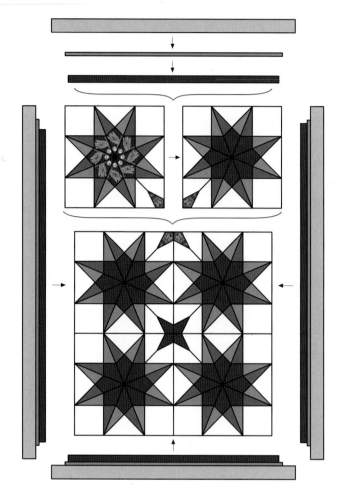

5. Layer the quilt top with batting and backing. Baste, quilt, bind, and label your quilt.

Other Applications for Mirrors

The first portion of this book concerned the manipulation of prints to create interesting and unique designs. But mirrors can be useful in a wide variety of other ways.

Orienting Blocks and Creating Secondary Designs

Set your mirrors at a 90° angle and place them along one corner of a block or block drawing. This will give you an idea of what the block will look like when repeated and set side by side. Would it look better turned in another direction?

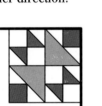

Double X Block with Mirrors at 90° on One Corner

Double X Block with Mirrors at 90° on Different Corner

Design Reflected in Mirrors

Design Reflected in Mirrors

Do interesting designs form where four blocks come together? If you are planning a multi-block quilt, you can preview the secondary shapes and designs that appear at the block intersections. Could these secondary designs be improved or highlighted by changing color placement or some of the design lines in your block? The mirrors may suggest some interesting possibilities. Experiment with tracing paper and colored pencils and you may discover ways to turn simple, traditional blocks into unique, original designs.

Remember that if your block is asymmetrical (or has a rotating pattern, such as a Pinwheel or Windmill block), the mirror image may be misleading. But if that mirror image is particularly intriguing, why not actually make some mirror-image blocks? By placing mirrors at a 90° angle on the corner of a Laced Star block, an interesting mirror-image design appears.

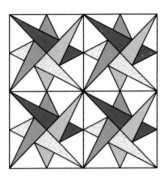

Laced Star
Normal Four-Block Repeat

Laced Star
Mirror-Image Design

Block Extension Design

To design your own unique blocks, place your mirrors on a block drawing, isolating a portion of it. The new reflected design expands the original design into a similar but larger, more complex block.

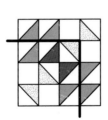
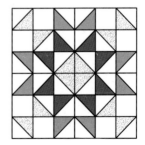

By placing mirrors at a 90° angle on three-fourths of the Ladies' Wreath block, I see a new block with a star design.

You may change the character of the original design completely. When I reflected three-fourths of a traditional block called Pennsylvania, a totally new design formed.

Placing the mirrors at a different point on the same traditional block, Pennsylvania, I created a totally different design.

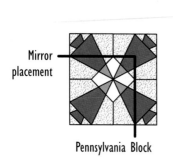

Mirror placement

Pennsylvania Block

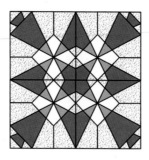

Pennsylvania Nights
Original Design Created
from Reflection

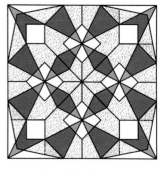

Mirror placement

Pennsylvania Block with
Different Mirror Placement

Franklin's Fantasy
Original Design Created
from Reflection

The new design contains a star shape. I named it Pennsylvania Nights. It looked somewhat three-dimensional to me, so I experimented with some color and value schemes to get transparent effects. The photo shows how this design might be interpreted in fabric.

To complete the interesting center design, I extended lines into the corners, then experimented with different ways to connect them. Remember that you are the designer and can take whatever liberties you want. You are limited only by your ability to piece what you design.

Feel free to add or remove lines to make a design simpler or more complex or to make piecing easier. With some designs, you may even see opportunities to incorporate the mirrored-print technique.

Generally, the more complex the block you start with, the more complex your extended design will be. For an even greater challenge, try extending your extended design. You can quickly design an entire quilt top with interesting shapes that merge or connect in unique and interesting ways.

This Pennsylvania Nights design was created by extending the Pennsylvania block. The values of the fabrics emphasize the three-dimensional look.

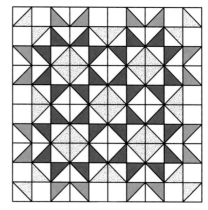

Design created by placing mirror on
⅚ of Ladies' Wreath Star Block

The centers of the star shapes are great places to use the mirrored-print technique.

Try setting your mirrors at a 60° angle and placing them at the upper midpoint of your block.

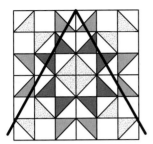

Ladies' Wreath Star with
Mirrors at 60° Angle

The resulting design is wonderful, though a bit harder to draft.

Star Wreath
Design Created by 60° Reflection of Ladies' Wreath Star Block

The best part about playing with the mirrors is that it's fast. You can rotate, repeat, and mirror-image blocks in an instant. Mirrors help you see traditional geometric designs in a whole new light. Experiment and have fun!

Designing Borders

This book is not meant to be a complete reference on borders. I assume that you either know the basics or can refer to one of the excellent books available on planning and designing borders, such as *Borders by Design* by Paulette Peters (That Patchwork Place). But I do hope to give you some ideas about using mirrors to plan the right border for your quilt.

Border Prints

If you are lucky enough to find a border print that coordinates with the mirror-print fabric in your blocks, you can use your mirrors to determine the best way for the border strips to meet at the corners.

For a square or rectangular quilt, the border-print strips will look best if they meet at a 45° angle in the mitered corners.

Place just one of your mirror tiles at a 45° angle to your border strip and slide it along the length of the strip. (Swing the tiles open until the wrong sides are facing each other and handle them as one piece.) Use a 45° triangle or template to check the exact angle of the mirrors. You will see what the design would look like if it stopped in the corner, turned 90°, and started up the side of the quilt.

Mirrors placed at a 45° angle on border stripes show potential corner treatments.

If all sides of the quilt are equal, and you have a symmetrical, nondirectional border print, you can achieve identical, mitered corners just by placing the same motif exactly in the center of each side of the quilt. (See the "Challenge Star" border on page 39.)

Most borders will require more planning. You may be able to manipulate the placement of your border motifs by making a seam in the center of the border strip. You could also work from the corners in, stopping a few inches from the center and piecing in a different central motif or design. With rectangular quilts, employ one of these methods if you want all four corners to look the same.

A great way to get the border-print motifs to fall where you want them is to make the quilt slightly larger by adding a plain spacer strip of fabric to the sides of the quilt before adding the final borders.

Some border prints are oriented in only one direction. Look at the heart-shaped motif below. It looks pleasing to have the two heart points meeting in the corner. But at the other ends of the border strips, the "fat" side of the hearts face up and won't form a corner like the one you just planned.

This mitered corner design forms when "points" face each other.

To remedy this, make a seam at the midpoint along each side of the quilt border to reverse the direction of the border stripe. All the corners can then be identical. With one-way directional prints, which are symmetrical from left to right, a center seam can look pleasing almost anywhere in the print, because when you cut and turn the print, it matches up in mirror-image fashion.

Reverse the direction of the print in the middle of the quilt sides to make corners uniform.

Analyze your border print to determine whether it is symmetrical and/or contains mirror images. Sometimes adjacent strips just reverse direction, and sometimes they are actually mirror-image prints.

Pieced Borders

Mirrors can help you decide how to turn the corner of a pieced border design. Draw several units of the design in a row on graph paper, to scale, leaving room above the row to represent the body of your quilt. Place a single side of your mirror tiles on the row of units at a 45° angle. The mirror shows a mitered corner, depicting how the pieced design would look turning the corner of the quilt. Slide the mirror slowly along the row until a pleasing design appears.

Feel free to alter the design you see in the mirrors by adding or subtracting design lines. Be aware of whether the corner design starts exactly at the completion of a border unit or not. You can turn the corner in the middle of a unit if you choose, as long as you plan the border so that a half unit lies at the correct position on each end.

Hidden Border Shapes

If you want something a little different from the traditional border shapes, experiment with your mirrors. Trace at least four repeats of your block design and set them in a four-patch configuration. Using a single side of the mirrors, slide it around the blocks, either at a 45° angle, straight up and down, or across. As the lines in the blocks connect with their mirror images, new shapes appear. You may see diamonds and trapezoids, for example, even though the blocks only contain triangles and squares. Or, you may see a combination of shapes that would not have occurred to you without the mirrors. Copy the shapes onto graph paper with a ⅛" grid and experiment to see if you can work them into a "unit repeat" size compatible with your quilt. Also, make sure that you can start and stop each row with the same design if you want your corners to be identical and symmetrical.

To experiment with the Kaleidoscope block, draw four blocks on graph paper and move the mirrors around the drawing.

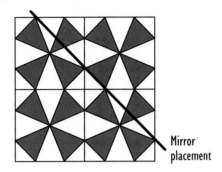

Place mirrors on group of Kaleidoscope blocks.

With the mirrors placed as in the drawing, the following shapes appear:

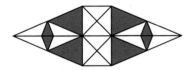

Using these shapes, I play around on my graph paper, keeping in mind that I want to end up with a repeating-unit size that will work easily with my quilt. The following ideas come to mind:

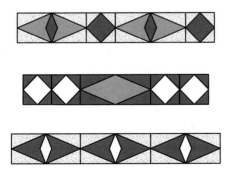

By placing mirrors at 45° on the last row, I find an interesting corner unit. Notice that the sides of my borders meet the end of the quilt at the midpoint of a unit.

Often a pieced border is made up of two or more different shapes. A border-unit repeat is measured from the beginning of a particular shape to the next beginning of the same shape. Some borders require an odd number of repeats in order to look balanced. Border shapes often look better in a smaller size than those in the quilt block. Keep in mind that intricately pieced borders may be too busy for your mirrored-print quilts, but they may look fabulous on a variety of other quilts.

Following are a few ideas for unusual borders, found by placing mirrors at various angles on traditional quilt blocks. Tracing four blocks together may yield even more designs, especially from the shapes at seams and block intersections. Experiment with a book of block designs. Or, if you have a quilt top that needs a border, draw the blocks and experiment with your mirrors. You may discover a hidden design to create that perfect one-of-a-kind border.

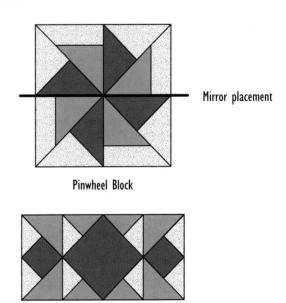

Pinwheel Block

Border Shapes Suggested

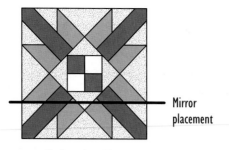

Mexican Star Block

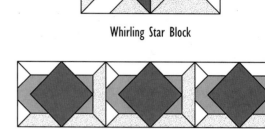

Whirling Star Block

Mirror placement

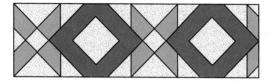

Border Shapes Suggested

Border Shapes Suggested

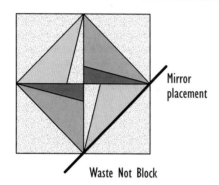

Mirror placement

Waste Not Block

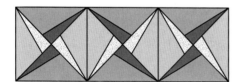

Border Shapes Suggested

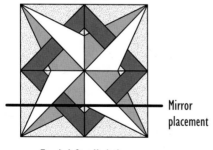

Mirror placement

Tangled Star Variation

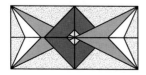

Border Shapes Suggested

Creating Your Own Quilting Designs

Once you've started using mirrors to manipulate printed and pieced designs, you may realize the limitless possibilities for new design ideas. Why not create some unique quilting designs?

There are plenty of commercial stencils available and books full of quilting designs. But you may not find exactly what you want or in the size and shape you need. With a little experimentation, you can adapt an existing design or create a totally new one.

Turning Corners

You may find a commercial border design that you like, but you don't know how to turn the corner, or you'd like to turn the corner in a different way or in a different portion of the design. Place the stencil on a large sheet of graph paper and align the design with the grid of the paper. (Translucent graph paper, from an art-supply store, can be used over a printed design.) Using a single side of the mirror, angle it at 45° (for a square or rectangular quilt) and move along the length of the design to find a pleasing "turning" point and a workable corner design.

(For a hexagonal quilt, place the mirrors at a 60° angle.) Once you have worked out the corner, you may need to adjust the length of the border-design repeat. Shorten or stretch it slightly, if necessary, to place your turning point at the corner where you want it. Be sure to distribute any adjustments among several repeats, so they won't be noticeable.

Triangular and Round Designs

The corner design that you have created may also be adaptable to a corner triangle, such as a setting block in a diagonally set quilt.

To create a circular design from a linear design or a single motif, use the hinged mirrors set at an angle (perhaps 60° or 45°), place them on the motif, and slide them back and forth until you see an interesting circular design.

Single Motif with Mirrors at 60° Angle

Slide tracing paper under the mirrors and mark along the bottom edges of the mirrors to mark the size of the wedge. Remove the mirrors and trace the design contained within the wedge shape. You don't have to use exactly what you see—pick and choose the interesting lines and shapes and alter them any way you want. You may select a wedge that will result in the finished circular size you need, but if you want your design to include details that would make the finished design too large, don't worry. You can reduce the design on a copy machine.

Once you have traced the wedge-shaped motif, make sure it is well defined. Draw the lines again with a fine-tip felt marker if they are too faint to be traced. Take a larger square of tracing paper and divide it into equal wedges. (If you used the mirrors at a 60° angle to isolate your design, you would divide the square into six equal 60° wedges; a 45° angle would require eight equal 45° wedges.)

Place the single wedge drawing under the larger tracing paper and trace the design onto each wedge.

Take any liberties you want in making the design flow smoothly from one wedge to the next. If the design is asymmetrical and you prefer to use the mirror-image design in adjacent wedges, simply turn your original drawing upside down for every other wedge.

Printed Fabric Motifs

One of my favorite sources for quilting designs is my fabric. You can use the motifs from the fabric in your quilt or from totally different fabric. The motifs may suggest wonderful designs, or you can use your mirrors to discover new combinations.

For the "Nosegay" quilt on page 37, I needed a large triangular quilting design for the corners. I set the mirrors at a 45° angle and moved them around the floral print I used in the quilt. An orchid and leaf design made an intriguing floral spray in the mirrors. I slipped tracing paper under the mirrors and traced the design.

Floral Design Traced into 45° Wedge

On a piece of tracing paper, I marked the size of a large corner triangle with 45° wedges dividing it. The actual size of the traced motif seemed to be in scale with my design, so I didn't reduce or enlarge it. I traced the design onto each of the four wedges.

Four wedge-shaped motifs are traced side by side.

For additional elements to extend into the corners and fill out the design, I went back to the print. I traced a calla lily and some leaves.

Slipping these drawings under my large tracing, I moved them around to see where they looked best. Then I traced them onto the larger design. On the right side, I turned the leaf drawing over to get a mirror image of the left side.

This traced design may be too busy.

At this point, the design looked too busy. Remember to balance the density and complexity of your quilting designs with the other design elements in your quilt. (Also consider whether it will take forever to quilt.)

To simplify the design, I deleted unnecessary lines and even some petals. When the design pleased me, I traced over it with a felt-tip marker and used a light box to transfer it to my quilt top.

The final design has been simplified.

Other Design Sources

Inspiration for quilting designs may come from a variety of sources. You may see interesting shapes and design elements in magazines or books, antique furniture, or architecture. Other stitchery projects, such as embroidery or appliqué, may contain designs that you could adapt. Floral designs on greeting cards or even wallpaper may suggest ideas. A bit of crocheted lace, an ornate picture frame, a favorite china pattern, the delicate scrollwork on a painted chest, the inlaid design on a jewelry box, even the design on a kitchen tile—designs are all around you. For a child's quilt, adapt animal shapes from a storybook or coloring book. Experiment and have fun using mirrors to personalize your quilts.

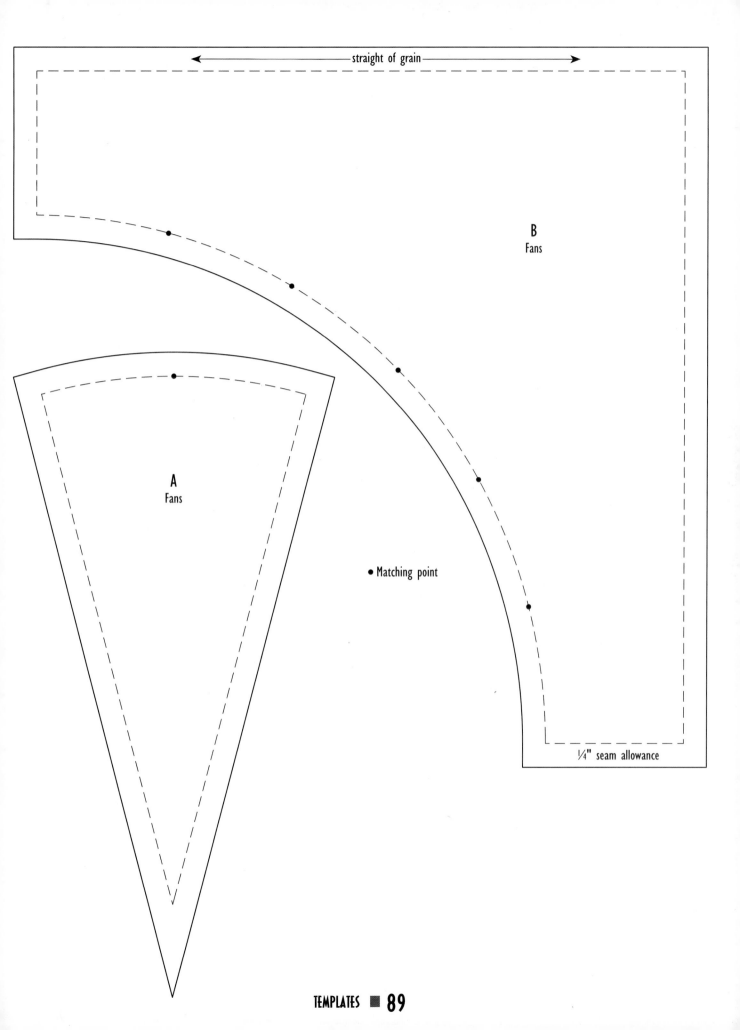

straight of grain

B
Fans

A
Fans

• Matching point

¼" seam allowance

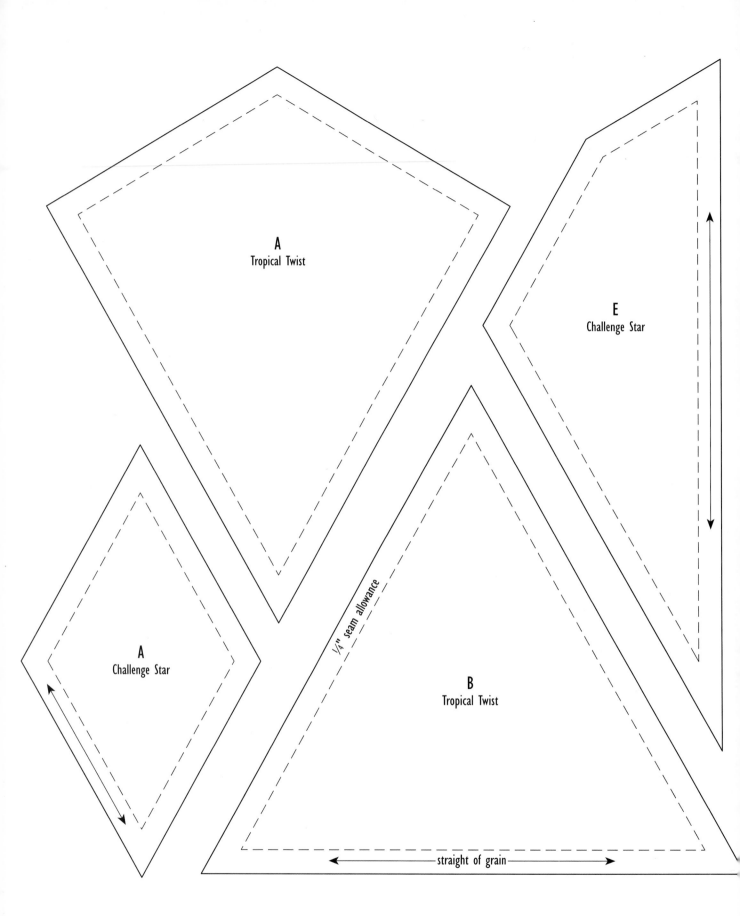

A
Tropical Twist

E
Challenge Star

A
Challenge Star

¼" seam allowance

B
Tropical Twist

straight of grain

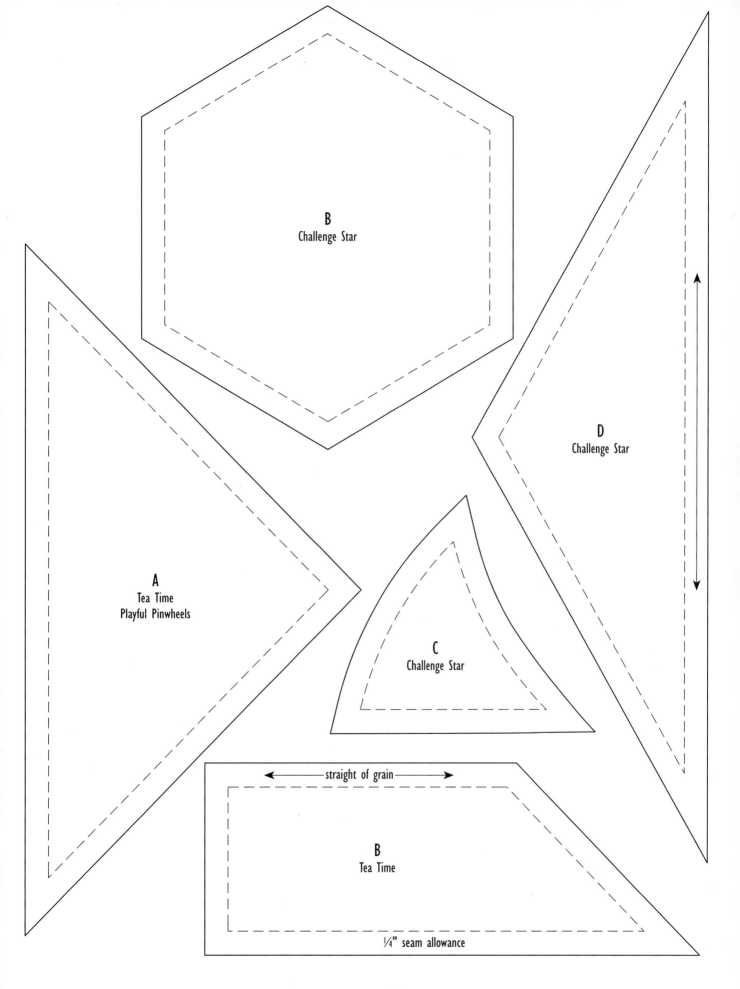

B
Challenge Star

D
Challenge Star

A
Tea Time
Playful Pinwheels

C
Challenge Star

straight of grain

B
Tea Time

¼" seam allowance

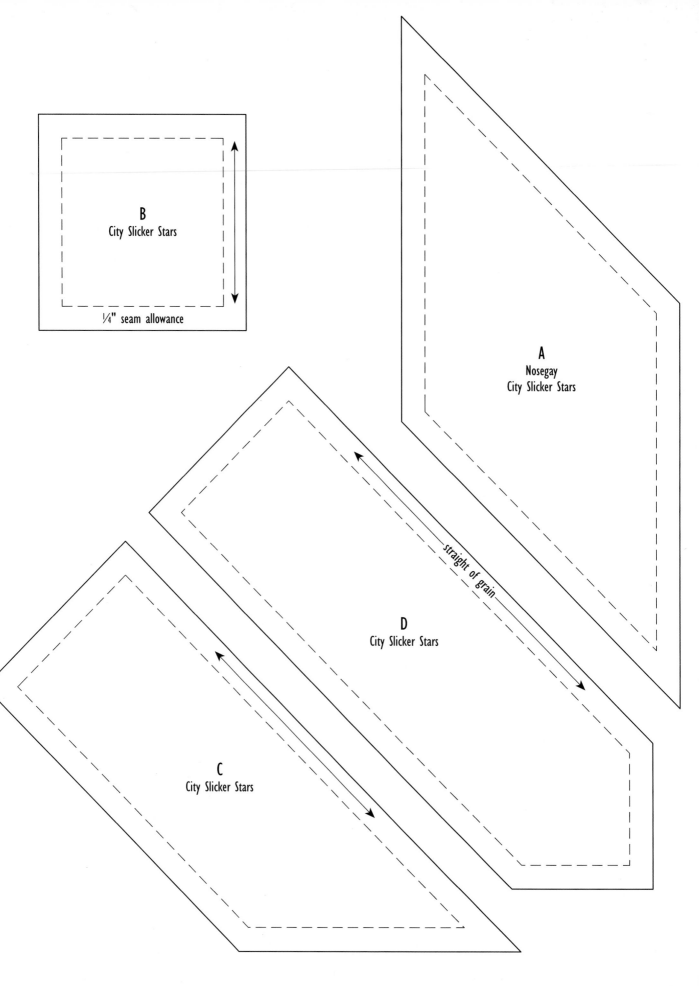

B
City Slicker Stars

¼" seam allowance

A
Nosegay
City Slicker Stars

straight of grain

D
City Slicker Stars

C
City Slicker Stars

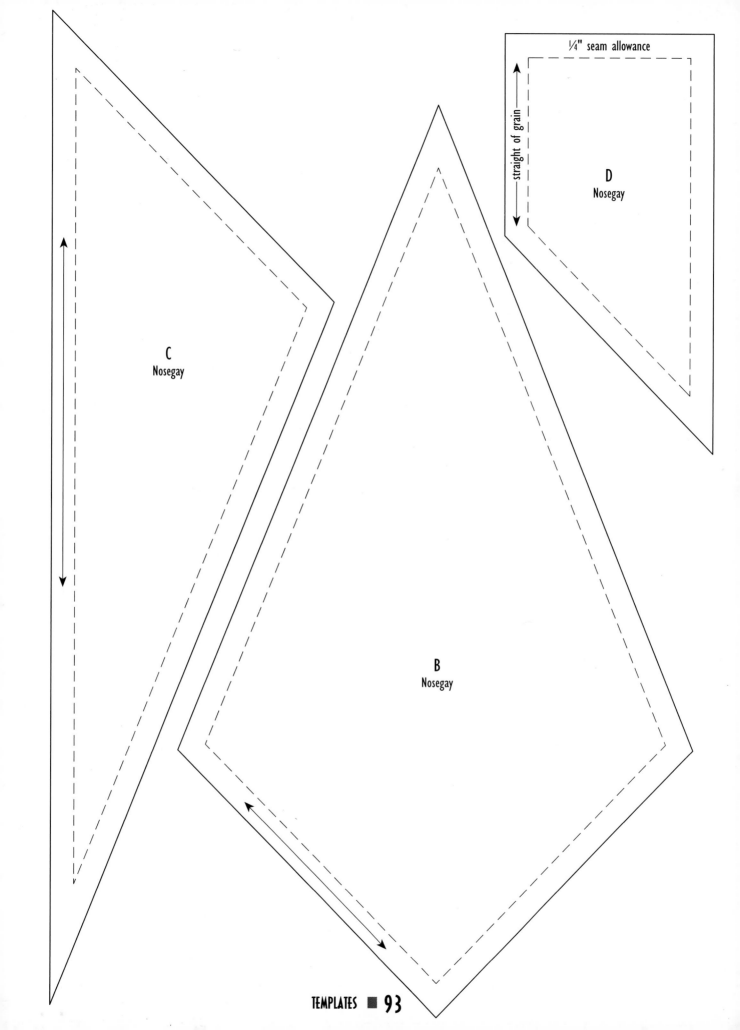

¼" seam allowance

straight of grain

D
Nosegay

C
Nosegay

B
Nosegay

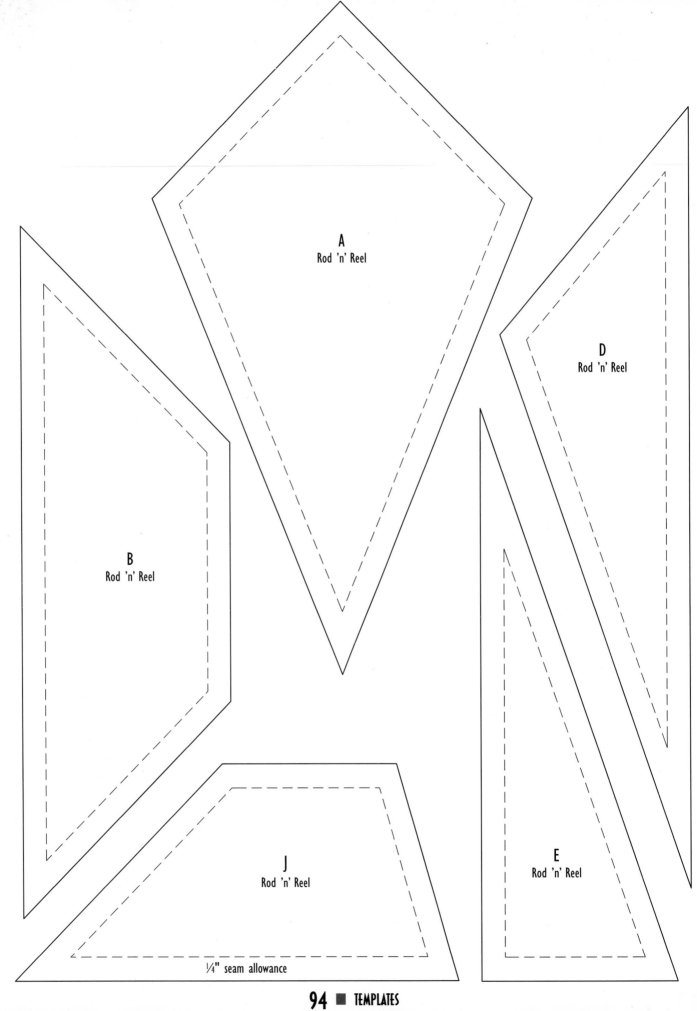

A
Rod 'n' Reel

B
Rod 'n' Reel

D
Rod 'n' Reel

E
Rod 'n' Reel

J
Rod 'n' Reel

¼" seam allowance

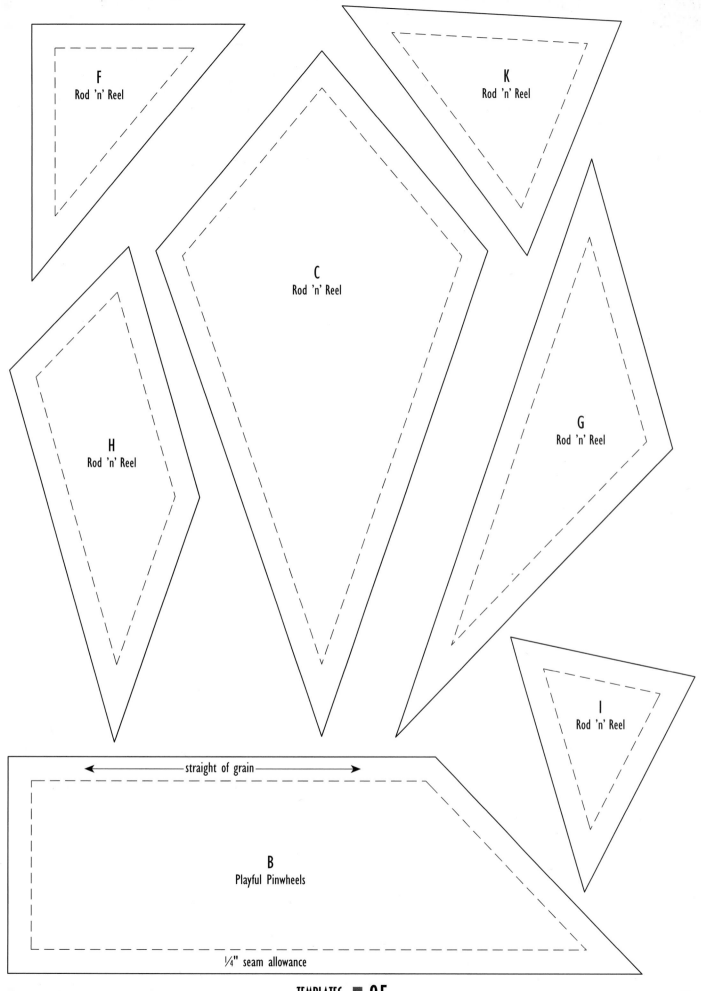

F
Rod 'n' Reel

K
Rod 'n' Reel

C
Rod 'n' Reel

H
Rod 'n' Reel

G
Rod 'n' Reel

I
Rod 'n' Reel

straight of grain

B
Playful Pinwheels

¼" seam allowance

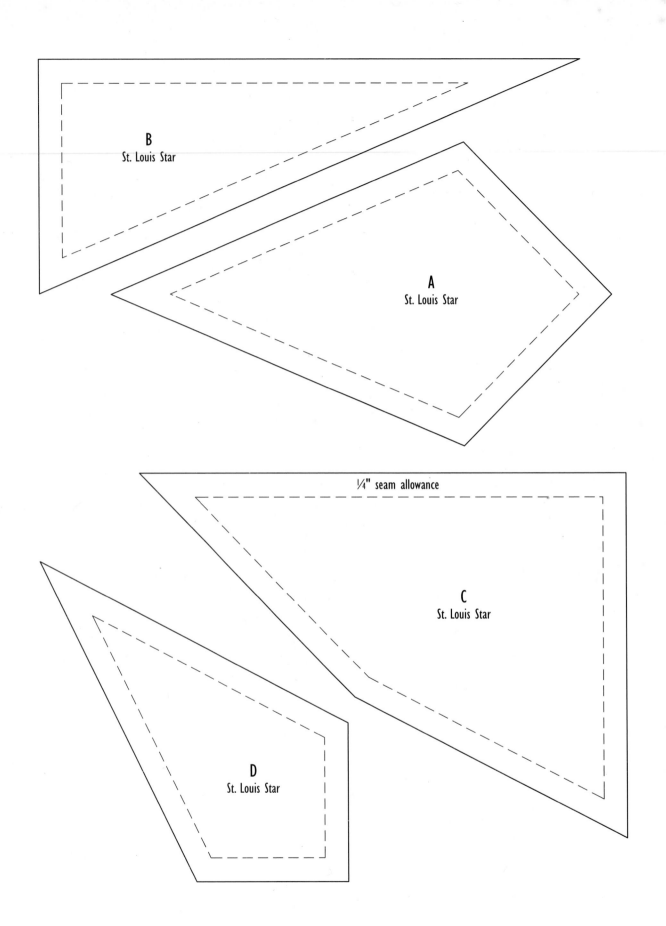

B
St. Louis Star

A
St. Louis Star

¼" seam allowance

C
St. Louis Star

D
St. Louis Star